WHO PAYS THE FERRYMAN?

Born of a maritime family, Roy Pedersen's former career with development agencies Highlands and Islands Development Board and Highlands and Islands Enterprise, where he pioneered numerous innovative and successful ventures, has given him a matchless insight into world shipping trends and into the economic and social conditions of the Highlands and Islands. He is now an author and the proprietor of a cutting-edge consultancy.

WHO PAYS THE FERRYMAN?

THE GREAT SCOTTISH FERRIES SWINDLE

Roy Pedersen

BIRLINN

First published in 2013 by
Birlinn Limited
West Newington House
10 Newington Road
Edinburgh
EH9 1QS

www.birlinn.co.uk

ISBN: 978 1 78027 122 4

British Library Cataloguing-in-Publication Data
A catalogue record for this book is available from the British Library

Typeset by Iolaire Typesetting, Newtonmore
Printed and bound by Grafica Veneta
www.graficaveneta.com

This book is dedicated to the memory of my father.
He opened my eyes to the world of shipping and boats.
His most precious gift: he taught me to think for myself.

CONTENTS

LIST OF ILLUSTRATIONS

Moss–Horten shuttle: a typical Norwegian *pendelferje*.

SeaLink Kangaroo Island 16-knot, 378-passenger, 55-car catamaran ferry *Sealion 2000*.

Foveaux Express arriving at Oban, the tiny capital of New Zealand's Stewart Island.

The first of ten new 49-metre Sea Transport Corporation 50-car ferries for the Philippines.

The Author and Professor Alf Baird being presented with best paper prize at the May 2012 STAR Conference.

FOREWORD

By Alfred Baird, Professor of Maritime Business,
Edinburgh Napier University

This book is a wonderful mix of history, economics, commercial success and failure, the latter so often nowadays associated with public sector (mis)management. Roy Pedersen provides an invaluable contribution to the ongoing story of Scotland's ferry industry. As a former officer with Highlands and Islands Enterprise and its predecessors, Roy has developed over the last 40 years and more an eye for what is good and what is bad about ferry services.

The historical perspective is provided for readers so that they might better understand how we have got to where we are today. We should not forget that Roy, as the inventor of Road Equivalent Tariff (RET), is well acquainted with the economics of ferry services. And here we see in full technicolor the interception of immense and ever-increasing subsidies for publicly run ferry operations in Scotland.

So, who intercepts these 'economic rents'? Well, the evidence presented tells us that the 'key stakeholders', namely the public operators, trade union members, local authorities, port trusts, and other vested interests intercept most of the subsidy long before what is left reaches the user. This leaves little for the benefit of users in terms. A case in point is the immense subsidy paid to Serco NorthLink to run its Pentland Firth service, only for users to express surprise when they find out that lower rates and a quicker, more frequent, passage can be obtained by using the unsubsidised Pentland Ferries service.

Roy Pedersen illustrates very clearly the difference in the competence of private ferry operators, most notably Western Ferries and Pentland Ferries, compared with the extraordinary inefficiencies of state-managed ferry operations and assets. The tragic consequence of this gross mismanagement brings him back to his former role at

HIE in helping island and remote communities improve their accessibility and through that to bring about a better chance to compete in whatever market. His identification of and preference for short ferry routes, where operators can offer higher levels of frequency at lower cost, and hence lower subsidy (or none), and ensure better accessibility, is compelling. The evidence on this from Western Ferries, Pentland Ferries and countless overseas operators is overwhelming. Yet the state, for the most part, continues to specify and is paying over the odds for the wrong routes and the wrong designs of ships and port facilities.

The cause is multi-facteted. Well-meaning civil servants 'responsible' for ferries start with limited knowledge of the sector, and take their advice from the vested interests. Ministers have even less knowledge, so take their advice from the officials. State-owned ferry entities are staffed by individuals who have limited commercial ferry expertise, or are from a military background where over-spending and over-specifying has been the norm.

If Roy Pedersen demonstrates anything, it is that the state should not be buying ferries, never mind operating them. The mistakes are endemic and long-term. A ship lasts 25 years or more, which implies that an expensive and inefficient ship will carry with it a significant financial burden for the same period.

The ongoing ferry fleet and port procurement activities sponsored by the state make the Edinburgh Tram debacle look like a very good deal indeed. And PFI is not dead; it lives on, not least in the newly ordered Stornoway ferry. And so long as a budget is made available for ferries, this tragedy will continue to be acted out, and vested interests will prevail.

Reform? How to do it? Roy Pedersen illustrates what can be done. The rather obvious solution is to shift to shorter routes, using less expensive vessels, which in turn allows for greater frequency, higher capacity and rising demand, and to leave ship procurement to people who at least understand what they are doing.

PREFACE

My parents met on a day cruise from Ardrossan to Rothesay on the old ex-Glasgow & South Western Railway turbine steamer *Atalanta*. In due course they married and I was born in an Ardrossan Harbour Board house as the Second World War was heading for Allied victory. I suppose I can attribute my existence to that Clyde steamer and the attractions of Rothesay.

One of my earliest memories, aged three, is a rough passage on Messrs Burns & Laird's fast and famous daylight boat *Lairds Isle* from Ardrossan to Belfast to visit relations. Then when I was four the family moved to Aberdeen where my father took up the post of Harbour Works Superintendent. Aberdeen harbour and its ships became my year-round playground, but we returned every summer to the Clyde Coast where steamer trips were always top priority. For several years from the age of thirteen, while my parents toured the Continent, I was lodged with my indulgent Aunt Peggy and given an 'Any Pier and Any Pier' season ticket to lose myself on the – then still substantial – fleet of railway steamers that plied the Firth. I wonder how many parents today would abandon their thirteen-year-old son, alone, to the vagaries of the railway and steamer timetable. Anyway, I'm glad they did and it's way too late now to call in the social services.

Distant Inveraray, Campbeltown, Arrochar and Tighnabruaich became as weel kent as the nearer joys of Brodick, Millport, Rothesay and Dunoon. So familiar were the ships, we boastful urchins of the Firth could identify them in seconds at two or three miles' distance; such is a boy's obsession. Happy days indeed.

Life and times moved on, but the fascination with matters maritime remained and, over the intervening years, I have been a keen observer and analyst of both the Scottish scene and comparators internationally. This book is in some small way a distillation of that experience.

ACKNOWLEDGEMENTS

The list of people who have contributed one way or another over many years to this work is a long one. Space does not permit mention of them all, but I am nonetheless grateful to everyone who has thrown light on the development of Scotland's ferries.

There are a number, however, I have to mention by name. First among these is Professor Alfred Baird, Head of the Maritime Research Group of Napier University's Transport Research Institute (TRI). His worldwide experience of shipping issues and his clear analytical mind have made an invaluable contribution.

I am grateful also to a wide range of ferry operators who have provided information at different periods on their vessels, and insights into their operational activities. Special thanks go to Gordon Ross, Managing Director of Western Ferries; Andrew and Susan Banks, owners of Pentland Ferries; Colin Manson, Resources Manager and Nina Croad, Ferry Services, Shetland Islands Council, Martin Gorringe, Marine Operations Manager at Argyll and Bute Council; Councillor John Laing, former chair of Highland Council TEC Services and Sam MacNaughton, Head of Transport and Infrastructure; Donald Ewen Darroch, Chairperson of the Overland Route Company Ltd; Stuart Ballantyne, CEO of Sea Transport Corporation; Craig Elder, Head of Strategy and Corporate Planning BC Ferries; Ian Munro, Managing Director of Stewart Island Marine Services; George Hudson, former Chairman of Fullers Ferries; Seumas Mackinnon, Misty Isle Boat Trips; Lyle White and Sunny Newitt of Brisbane CityFerries; Peter Wotherspoon of Jura Ferry; Duncan McEachran, Kerrera ferry; David Cannon and the late Colin Patterson, former CEO of Caledonian MacBrayne.

Among officials in public bodies who provided useful information, I must thank Guy Platten of CMAL; Dave Duthie and Ranald Robertson of HITRANS; Tony Usher, General Manager of Highland Council Harbours Authority; and Colin Grieve and Judith Ainslie in Transport Scotland. I would also like to thank Howie Firth for facilitating the CO2 presentation at the Orkney Science Festival and Ian Mathie of SES-TRAN for information about the North Berwick – Anstruther ferry. Among the many other individuals who have provided advice, inspiration or data, thanks are due to Bill Banks; Arthur Blue; Councillor Jim Foubister; Catrina Howard, Marketing Coordinator, SeaLink – South Australia; Harold Jordan; James Knight; Bill Mowat; John Mowat; Hugh Raven; Uisdean Robertson; John Rose; Duncan Swinbanks; Captain Torgeir H. Røyset; Steven Watson; 'Scotships' correspondents; and my second cousin and naval architect Øyvind Wilhelmsen.

Numerous websites have been referred to – too many to be listed, had a list actually been kept. Three deserve special mention, however, for the comprehensiveness of information contained. These are www.shipsofcalmac.co.uk; www.shetland.gov.uk/ferries; and www.bcferries.com.

Finally I must once again thank Marie Kilbride who kindly agreed to proofread the text in the pursuit of accuracy. With regard to that aim, the final responsibility rests with me. If any errors are found, then the fault is mine alone.

Roy Pedersen, Inverness, May 2013

LIST OF ABBREVIATIONS

AB – able seaman
BC – British Columbia, Canada
BR – British Railways, later British Rail
BTC – British Transport Commission
CalMac – Caledonian MacBrayne
CMAL – Caledonian Marine Assets
CO_2 – carbon dioxide
CPR – Canadian Pacific Railway
CSPCo – Caledonian Steam Packet Company
CV – commercial vehicle
DMG – David MacBrayne Group
GPK&A – Glasgow Paisley Kilmarnock & Ayr Railway
GSWR – Glasgow & South Western Railway
HFO – heavy fuel oil
HIDB – Highlands and Islands Development Board
HIE – Highlands and Islands Enterprise
HITRANS – Highlands and Islands Transport Partnership
IC – internal combustion (engine)
IMO – International Maritime Organisation
KIMO – Kommunenes Internasjonale Miljøorganisasjon or
    Local Authorities International Environmental Organisation
km/h – kilometres per hour
LMS – London Midland & Scottish Railway
LNER – London & North Eastern Railway
LNG – liquefied natural gas
MCA – Maritime and Coastguard Agency
mph – miles per hour
MRF – Møre og Romsdal Fylkesbåter
MSP – Member of the Scottish Parliament

OIC – Orkney Islands Council
Pax – passengers (numbers)
RET – road equivalent tariff
RIB – reinforced inflatable boat
RMT – National Union of Rail, Maritime and Transport Workers
RoPax – RO-RO vehicle and passenger (vessel)
RO-RO – roll-on/roll-off (ferry)
SEA – Strategic Environmental Assessment
SIC – Shetland Islands Council
SMT – Scottish Motor Traction Company
SNP – Scottish National Party
SOLAS – International Convention for Safety of Life at Sea
STAG – Scottish Transport Appraisal Guidance
STG – Scottish Transport Group
TEU – twenty-foot equivalent (container) unit (a measure of
  container ship capacity)
TUC – Trades Union Congress
WA – Washington State, USA

INTRODUCTION

When my book *Pentland Hero* was published in 2010, it caused something of a sensation. It told of how Andrew Banks, a quietly spoken Orkney farmer's son and his tiny team of trusted colleagues, without a penny of public funds, started operating Pentland Ferries on a new frequent, cheap, short sea ferry crossing between Orkney and the Scottish mainland. The enterprise has been a huge success despite predatory competition from the heavily subsidised NorthLink, a misguided and wasteful national ferry policy and a sustained official campaign to undermine his efforts.

Then the announcement that the Scottish Government intended to undertake a 'route and branch' review of Scotland's internal ferry operations was an occasion for celebration. It was hoped that the injustice with which Andrew and others had been treated would have been addressed and a more cost-effective national policy adopted. In the event, sadly, the plan that emerged was a disappointment. There were a few enhancements, but little attempt to tackle the underlying inefficiencies.

It is against that background that this book continues the theme of Scottish coastal maritime entrepreneurship on a Scotland-wide canvas. It describes the main players in the current provision of ferry and coastal passenger services. It highlights how half of Scotland's ferry traffic is handled by efficient and innovative commercial operators while the other half is in the hands of a public sector that in some instances swallows up scandalous and world-beating amounts of public funds while providing an indifferent service.

How this came to pass was the result of changing economic, technological and political forces over not just decades, but centuries. The effects of these forces, good and bad, are examined, as are the growing environmental problems associated with the state-controlled ferry sector.

There are other countries where things are done differently in terms of better ferry services for less money. Norway, British Columbia, Australia and New Zealand in particular have cracked many of the issues that bedevil Scotland's state-funded ferry operations. These exemplars are examined and lessons drawn.

Finally, as an antidote to the present inadequacies of Scotland's national ferry policies, an analysis is set out as to how ferry operations could be organised and developed so as to provide much improved access to our island and peninsular communities, to aid their economic and social development, while actually reducing costs and environmental impact.

CHAPTER 1

THE SCENE

From our vantage point we take in the sweep of the bay sheltered behind the rocky headland. It is topped by some old fortification. On the horizon to seaward we can make out the blue-grey outline of distant hills. The scudding clouds throw moving shadows across a choppy sea. It's a pleasing scene. The sun bursts through a widening gap in the clouds and suddenly shooting out from behind the headland appears a ferry brightly bathed in sunlight. She is heading purposefully into the bay, white feathers of spray rising from her bows and a creaming wake behind her.

Soon she is slowed, swung and berthed at the terminal. Cars, vans, cycles and passengers stream ashore. After a time, a fresh load of passengers and vehicles is taken onboard and she is off again to disappear behind the headland.

This is a ritual that can be witnessed daily in dozens of Scottish coastal and island locations. The ritual is part of the very fabric of island life; the means by which supplies are imported, local produce is exported, and business, social and leisure contacts are maintained. And, of course, the business of tourism generates wealth in many a community.

It was Sir Walter Scott who really sparked off Scotland's tourist trade. He opened the minds of the world to the romance of Scotland's story set against its dramatic backdrop – Caledonia stern and wild. And who can deny the allure of our coastal landscape? In fact, Scotland has the world's second most indented coastline,[1] featuring long sea lochs, firths and extended peninsulas. This, coupled with a rocky mountainous terrain and the ever-changing light and weather, accounts for the country's magical and at times breathtaking scenery. This magical quality is further enhanced by the 790 or so islands and islets that

[1] It is Norway that has the world's most indented coastline.

lie off the Scottish coast. Of these 94 are populated, with just under 100,000 inhabitants in total. Four inhabited islands are found on inland freshwater lochs.

Most of the inhabited islands, a number of peninsulas and loch-side communities are linked to the mainland communication network by 145 public ferry connections, a number of which operate in summer only. Four run between Scottish ports and places outwith Scotland. Well over a hundred vessels make up this fleet. They vary in size from small open boats, as at Easdale, to very large multi-deck passenger- and vehicle-carrying roll-on/roll-off ships, as in the service between Cairnryan and Northern Ireland. Of the total number, 57 are vehicle ferry crossings. The fleet is run by no fewer than 46 separate concerns varying in size from the largest, Caledonian MacBrayne Ferries with 30 ships, to self-employed operators with a single small vessel.

A huge corpus of literature, both fact and fiction, exists on the subject of Scottish islands, much of which presents a romanticised view of island life. By the same token a romanticised view of Scottish ferries has been generated on the back of the written word. In fact a sizeable library could be filled with books on Scottish coastal shipping. Quite a number are works of real scholarship and careful research, read avidly by a surprisingly large following of enthusiasts. It is the ships themselves, their stations and their operating companies that are perhaps of primary interest for the majority of authors. The ships of the Clyde, its firth and the West Highlands and Islands dominate the corpus; those of Orkney and Shetland come next, with relatively little on the maritime heritage of the east coast and its firths.

In truth, there is romance in the tale, for the Scottish coastal passenger fleets of today are the culmination of a maritime heritage that stretches back almost to the end of the last ice age, some 10,000 years ago, when humans moved coastward into what is now Scotland. To help convey an understanding of how we got from then to now, I will say something later about the evolution of coastal shipping in the context of the political, economic and technological circumstances prevailing at different historical periods.

It is, however, the ferry in its modern manifestation and its social, political, economic, technological and environmental context that is the main focus of this book. Until about the 1970s the term 'ferry' was generally understood as a broad-beamed vessel shuttling to and fro across a river, loch or narrow coastal sound. Over the previous century and a half, a powered vessel undertaking any longer passage on a schedule was invariably referred to as a 'steamer', even if latterly propelled by internal combustion machinery rather than steam.

For the purposes of this book I have taken as a definition of a ferry: a vessel shipping and landing passengers, and in many cases vehicles, on a regular schedule between two or more ports. In most such cases where vehicles are carried, they are driven on and off the vessel at any state of the tide, at specially constructed terminals, equipped either with link-spans (hinged bridges connecting ferry to shore) or with inclined slipways. The system is known as 'roll-on/roll-off' or RO-RO for short. The designs of ferry and of terminal are many and varied.

There is another fleet operating with passengers in Scottish coastal and inland waters that is important to mention. This fleet offers pleasure cruises. These vary in scope from extended cruises by massive cruise liners to short non-landing excursions by local small boat operators. Each contributes in its own way to the Scottish tourism economy, and there is inevitably some overlap between the ferry and cruise business. While not the main subject of this book, cruising is worthy of some consideration as part of the overall context.

Before looking in more detail at Scotland's ferry operations and how well or otherwise they perform their allotted tasks, one significant point should be borne in mind. In the nineteenth century Scotland led the world in ship design, in shipbuilding, marine engineering and ship owning. The twentieth century witnessed the gradual demise of that pre-eminence, until today Scotland barely reaches the 'also ran' category. That is not to deny there are some very innovative and efficient ferry operations to be found around Scotia's shores. Sadly, these are countered by much that is highly inefficient, environmentally damaging, costly to the taxpayer and propped up by decades of wrong-headed public policy.

It is quite a tall order to describe and analyse, in this one small volume, the great range and variety of Scotland's ferry services. To ease the task all routes are tabulated in Appendix 1. The list moves from south to north round the coast, starting in the south-west, indicating in each case the passage length in kilometres, the operator, the annual carryings of passengers, and vehicles conveyed annually on each route (where available). Appendix 2 is a fleet list by operator of ferry vessels engaged on regular service in Scottish waters with the routes on which

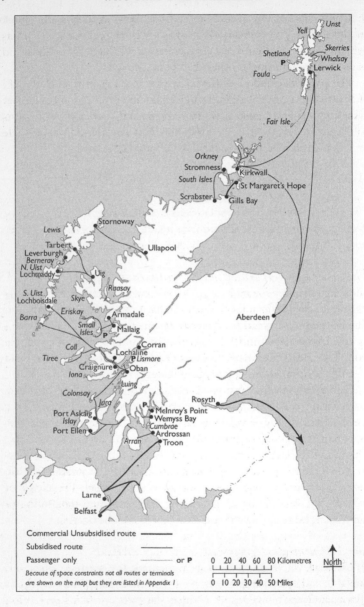

Scottish Vehicle Ferry Routes

they normally operate. The term 'vehicle ferry' as used in this book should generally be understood as one conveying passengers as well as vehicles. By the same token a 'passenger ferry' should be understood as not conveying vehicles other than perhaps cycles.

The pages that follow will explore who is doing what in the world of Scottish ferries, how this all came about and what is good and what is bad. Drawing on good practice at home and overseas, suggestions will be advanced as to how a better, more cost-effective and sustainable arrangement for running Scottish ferries can be realised.

THE REGULATORY SYSTEM

The range of Scottish ferry operations is a varied one. Whether large or small, operators have to function within a legal and regulatory framework as administered by various bodies. These are:

The International Maritime Organization (IMO)

Shipping accounts for more than 90 per cent of world trade. There is a need, therefore, for international standards to regulate the industry. The first maritime treaties date from the nineteenth century, but it was the loss of the *Titanic* in 1912 that brought about the first international Safety of Life at Sea, or SOLAS, convention. This remains the most important treaty addressing maritime safety.

The IMO is a United Nations agency, established in 1948. Its main task has been to develop and maintain a regulatory framework for shipping and especially safety, environmental concerns, legal matters, technical cooperation, maritime security and the efficiency of shipping. The IMO is based in London and, among its many responsibilities, it lays out measures aimed at the prevention of accidents, including standards for ship design, construction, equipment, operation and manning. Prevention of pollution by ships is now a major focus. Inspection and monitoring of compliance, however, are the responsibility of member states.

The Maritime and Coastguard Agency (MCA)

At UK level, the MCA is the body responsible for maritime safety and standards under the framework of the IMO conventions. The MCA provides a search and rescue service, enforces ship safety, pollution prevention and seafarer well-being through registration and inspection.

All seagoing vessels registered in the UK are assigned to a specific class, which defines their permitted use, determines which certification they must hold and specifies the inspection and survey regime required. For many years, the classes of passenger ships engaged on various types of voyage have been:

Class I – Long international voyages

Class II – International voyages of less than 24 hours

Class II (A) – Domestic voyages, which are not ships of Classes III to VI(A)

Class III – Voyages not more than 70 miles by sea from their point of departure and not more than 18 miles from the coast of the UK and only in favourable weather and during restricted periods

Class IV – Vessels operating in partially smooth waters

Class V – Vessels operating in smooth waters

Class VI – Not more than 250 passengers on board, in favourable weather and during restricted periods, not more than 15 miles from the point of departure, nor more than 3 miles from land

Class VI (A) – Carrying not more than 50 passengers for a distance of not more than 6 miles. Voyages to or from isolated communities on the islands or coast of the UK and which do not proceed for a distance of more than 3 miles from land

These traditional classifications are now being replaced by European classifications. Vessels carrying twelve or fewer passengers do not require a passenger certificate, but must of course comply with other rules. Certification covers such matters as: minimum safe manning, passenger safety, dangerous goods, probable wave heights, air pollution and permitted areas of operation.

So long as operators comply with the requirements of the MCA and with any other legal obligations, ferry and cruise operators are free to ply their trade for hire and reward as and where they wish.

Tendering Ferry Services

Things get more complicated when public funds are used to subsidise ferry services. Under European state aid rules, public authorities are required to offer the routes proposed for subsidy to competitive tender. Some local authorities that run ferry services in their areas seem to have avoided tender services by testing the efficiency of services on a 'best value' basis. Other individual routes are simply put out to tender in the same manner as a bus contract. The winning contractor is paid an agreed annual sum to run the route for, usually, six years in accordance with the timetable, fares and other requirements set out in the contract.

When it comes to the Scottish Government, the process of tendering ferry services is infinitely more convoluted. There has been no overriding rationale as to which actual routes are to be supported by the Scottish Government other than historical accident. As will be illustrated in the following pages, the procedure in place for state funding of ferry services is deeply flawed and has over the years led to some astounding, inefficient, environmentally damaging and highly expensive outcomes. The main influencers of the process are:

1. The Scottish Government (politicians and officials), through Transport Scotland, which sets the policy for the government-supported routes, sets the specifications for the routes to be tendered and pays the subsidies
2. Local authorities (politicians and officials) and community groups, which seek to influence policy and specification on government-supported routes in their area
3. The state-owned operators of the David MacBrayne Group, namely Caledonian MacBrayne Ferries, Argyll Ferries and until recently NorthLink Ferries who are keen (some may say desperate) to hold on to the routes they operate and to influence policy to achieve that end
4. State-owned CMAL (Caledonian Maritime Assets Ltd) who own the ferries and many terminals for lease to the David MacBrayne Group
5. The unions, who favour the bloated status quo to 'protect' ferry jobs and unusually generous conditions

THE OPERATORS

Scottish ferry operators can be classified under two important headings: those who operate on a commercial basis without subsidy, and those who receive subsidy from the public purse.

Commercial Operators

In overall terms, Scotland's commercial operators (excluding visiting cruise liners) account for about half the passengers and cars, and over two thirds of the freight, conveyed on Scotland's ferries. All this is carried out without subvention from the taxpayer. This means that the tendering rules to not apply to commercial operators.

These cover a wide range. In the south-west Western Ferries' single route between Hunter's Quay (Cowal) and McInroy's Point (Inverclyde) is Scotland's busiest in terms of passengers and cars carried. Stena Line's Cairnryan–Belfast service with *Stena Superfast VII* and *Stena Superfast VIII* employs the biggest ships and comes second in ranking after Western Ferries in terms of passengers and cars. P&O Ferries with their conventional 'Superferries' *European Causeway* and *European Highlander* running between Cairnryan and Larne top the bill in terms of numbers of commercial vehicles/trailers carried. In summer, P&O also operate Scotland's fastest ferry, the 40-knot Incat catamaran, *Express*, alternately between Larne and Cairnryan or Troon.

Further north, Highland Council operates Scotland's second busiest ferry in terms of cars, across the Corran narrows. Operating costs are fully met from farebox revenue. And Pentland Ferries' catamaran *Pentalina* now carries the majority of cars across the Pentland Firth between Caithness and Orkney against heavily subsidised competition.

The east coast hosts two important freight operators. DFDS run thrice weekly between Rosyth and Zeebrugge; sadly, this route no longer caters for passengers and cars. Streamline Shipping, while not strictly speaking a ferry operation, provides a container service between Aberdeen and Orkney and Shetland.

Besides the major commercial vehicle ferry operators, there are a host of unsubsidised passenger and cruise operations varying from considerable fleets like Cruise Loch Lomond, Sweeny's Cruises and Maid of the Forth, to local single boat owners. These collectively make a significant contribution to Scotland's economy.

There is undoubtedly an overlap between the humdrum role of a public scheduled ferry and pleasure cruising. Indeed, many ferry trips are regarded as mini-cruises by travellers. Over and above the business of ferry operation, quite a number of the commercial operators, particularly those who operate the smaller class of vessel, also operate non-ferry cruises, hires or non-landing excursions which do not, of course, qualify, in the strict sense, as ferry runs.

Lest it be thought a frivolity to include so many small boat operators within the list of 'big time' operators, one example may serve to put things in perspective. The motor launches that undertake the ferry run between Elgol (Skye) and remote Loch Coruisk offer almost as much daily passenger capacity (1,080) in summer as on the NorthLink Aberdeen–Orkney–Shetland route (1,200). When it is borne in mind that the Loch Coruisk trips cost the taxpayer nothing, but do much to retain visitors in Skye, whereas the Aberdeen service costs the taxpayer some £350 per round-trip passenger, it gives pause for thought.

Space does not allow mention of the numerous boat trip operators to be found right around the Scottish coasts. They vary from increasingly popular wildlife-watching excursions, to fast RIB thrill-seeker forays, to more extended and sedate sleep-aboard cruises by operators like the Majestic Line's 80-foot (24-metre) vessels *Glen Massan* and the *Glen Tarsan* with accommodation for up to 11 guests in 6 double cabins.

On a larger and more luxurious scale is *Hebridean Princess*; the former MacBrayne car ferry *Columba*, operated by Hebridean Island Cruises, carries up to 50 guests on cruises of between four and ten nights to the West Highlands and Islands, St Kilda, Orkney and Shetland. Another cruise ship catering for the luxury end of the market is the *Lord of the Glens* operated by the Magna Carta Steamship Company Ltd. She is designed both to fit the locks of the Caledonian Canal and to navigate the open sea.

Each of the above sleep-aboard vessels are of a size that can reach small, interesting and picturesque places inaccessible to larger cruise ships. In terms of annual clients catered for, however, they are tiny in scale when compared with the big international cruise liner business.

Indeed, as a cruise destination, Scotland is increasingly popular with an international clientele. Among the Scottish ports with frequent calls are Greenock, Oban, Fort William, Portree, Ullapool, Stornoway, Scrabster, Kirkwall, Lerwick, Invergordon, Peterhead, Aberdeen and Leith. It is a feature of the trade that, at times, large numbers of clients landed at some of the smaller communities from a big cruise liner can stretch local transport, heritage and retail facilities, but by and large the business is a welcome boost to local economies. Very often calls at Scottish ports are but part of wider itineraries covering other British and Irish ports, transatlantic repositioning, or combined with cruises to the Faeroe Islands, Iceland or the Norwegian fjords, the Baltic or continental Europe.

Visiting cruise liners brought in around £41 million to the Scottish economy in 2012. Aside from public investment in some shore facilities, the industry is wholly commercial and unsubsidised, generating international profile, local wealth, employment and tax revenues.

Subsidised Operators

The operators who are supported by subventions either by the Scottish Government or local authorities present a different and varied picture.

By far the largest, most heavily subsidised and perhaps best known operator is Caledonian MacBrayne Ferries, also known as CalMac, a subsidiary of the David MacBrayne Group (DMG). This state-owned operator runs a fleet of 30 ships on 24 routes on the Firth of Clyde and the West Highlands and Islands. The ships and a number of terminals at which the ships berth are owned by the separate state-owned entity Caledonian Maritime Assets Ltd, or CMAL, and leased to the operating company. With a few exceptions the ships are of two types, namely, 9 or 10 large, expensive-to-operate class IIA (that is to say rough water) RO-RO ferries varying in capacity from 50 to 120 cars and approximately 500 to 1,000 passengers; and a fleet of smaller more economical double-ended 'Loch-class' vessels varying in capacity from 12 to 36 cars, 150 to 250 passengers and designed to operate to slipways. Another subsidiary of the DMG is Argyll Ferries which operates two passenger-only ferries between Dunoon (Cowal) and Gourock (Inverclyde).

In 2011–12 the revenue from CalMac and Dunoon fares, catering, etc. was £58.7 million, to which was added an astonishing total net Scottish Government subsidy of £70.3 million, being £76 million grant less a claw-back of £5.7 million.

The next largest subsidy goes to NorthLink which runs vehicle ferries between Aberdeen and Kirkwall (Orkney) and Lerwick (Shetland) and also across the Pentland Firth between Scrabster (Caithness) and Stromness (Orkney). In 2012, Serco, the international service company, won the six-year Northern Isles contract. The Scottish Government annual subsidy is £40.5 million for the two routes.

A number of local authorities also use public money to fund ferry services. The biggest spender in this regard is Shetland Islands Council which has, after CalMac, numerically Scotland's second largest ferry fleet of 12 vessels, operating from 16 terminals serving 8 islands. The council has a policy of early-till-late operating hours and very low fares. In the case of Bluemull Sound the service is free for all passengers, cars and light commercials. The total annual revenue receipts for Shetland's internal ferries are £1.75 million, supplemented by a subsidy of £13.5 million.

Next in descending order of subsidy is Orkney Ferries, owned by Orkney Islands Council, running a fleet of nine inter-island ferries. The subsidy for 2010–11 was circa £6.2 million against revenue from fares, catering, etc. of £2.4 million.

Highland Council's financial support for ferry services is modest. As already mentioned, the busy council-run Corran ferry is operated on a cost-recovery basis, and as such is not subsidised, Three other routes are tendered out to private operators, for which the total subsidy paid in 2012 was £278,000. This was broken down as follows: Camasnagaul at £80,000, Inverie at £158,000 and Cromarty at £40,000.

Argyll and Bute Council operate a vehicle ferry to the island of Luing and the Port Appin to Point (Lismore) passenger ferry. It also contracts the passenger ferry between Seil and Easdale; the vehicle ferry operation between Port Askaig (Islay) and Feolain (Jura); and in the short term, a fast 12-passenger RIB in summer between Craighouse (Jura) and Tayvallich (Knapdale).

Strathclyde Passenger Transport subsidy to the Gourock–Kilcreggan ferry route operated by Clydelink is approximately £190,000 per annum.

THE SUBSIDY MOUNTAIN

The irony is that when Caledonian MacBrayne was created in 1973, as a subsidiary of the then Scottish Transport Group (STG), the original ambition was that the company would operate as a commercial concern, covering its costs from farebox revenue. It wasn't long, however, before excuses were made as to why things were not working to plan. The begging bowl was out and the company needed an ongoing subsidy to keep it afloat.

The STG Annual Report and Accounts for 1975 set out the gross revenue (that is, turnover plus government grant) for its shipping and haulage operations as £10 million. However, a deficit before government grant was posted of £3,245,000 (about £21 million at 2010 values) or 32 per cent of gross revenue. This amount was covered by subsidy of a broadly similar amount. That report broke the deficit down into broad geographical areas of operation, a reporting feature never to be repeated by the STG for the rest of its existence.

Ten years later after a period of chronic inflation, the 1985 report showed what appeared to be a slightly improving position, with gross revenue of £22.34 million and a deficit of £3,792,000 (about £16 million at 2010 values) or 30 per cent of costs. Then the 1986 report revealed that: 'over the last six years the Government has helped Caledonian MacBrayne fund new investment totalling some £22 million for vessels and nearly £7 million for terminals'; this did not include financing costs. If these capital sums were spread evenly over the six-year period the subsidy to cover the deficit would amount to no less than some 52 per cent of revenue – for a company that ten years earlier was supposed to operate as a self-financing commercial concern.

With the privatisation of the STG's bus interests, the company was wound up in 1993, by which time Caledonian MacBrayne had been spun off as a separate state-owned company under the direct control, initially, of the Secretary of State for Scotland and, after devolution, of Scottish ministers.

There was little change until the convoluted process of tendering commenced around the turn of the millennium. The 2003 CalMac accounts indicated that the company received a subsidy of £18.9 million, about 31 per cent of its operating expenditure of £61.9 million. This equates to 23 per cent of gross revenue but did not take account of capital grants. This was partially rectified in 2004 when subsidy had increased substantially to £25.9 million (about £31 million at present values) or around 30 per cent of gross revenue.

Then the subsidy really started to climb. By 2007–08 it had reached £38.3 million, or 39 per cent of gross revenue and, according to Cal-Mac's Annual Report and Accounts for 2011–12, it was £69.3 million or 54 per cent of gross revenue, one reason being the introduction of leasing charges for vessels by CMAL. That means that for the first time the level of subsidy to Caledonian MacBrayne Ferries was significantly greater than the farebox revenue.

If that seems shocking, the performance of NorthLink in its last year of state ownership was even worse, where the net subsidy of £43 million represented a staggering 61 per cent of the £70 million gross revenue. Although the exact split in losses between NorthLink's Pentland Firth and Aberdeen services is not revealed, a 25 per cent to 75 per cent split is believed to be close to the mark. This equates to subsidies of some £150 and an astonishing £350 per round-trip passenger respectively.

So far as has been ascertained, Scottish Government funding for ferries operated by the David MacBrayne Group and NorthLink combined is the world's highest. It is surely worrying that at a time when public finances are constrained, the horn of plenty never seems to diminish for the DMG, when the money could be more advantageously utilised for the development of our peripheral communities. The profligacy is especially frustrating when many independent Scottish ferry and cruise operators undertake their business on an efficient, profitable commercial basis without any recourse to subsidy at all.

Although subsidies have risen to very high levels, traffic growth is sluggish. A contributory factor to this state of affairs is that even many of the newer vessels employed are of old-fashioned design and are otherwise less than optimal for their purpose. On longer, open sea (Class IIA or European Class B) routes, CalMac developed relatively large roll-on/roll-off (RO-RO) ferries that are expensive to build (currently circa £25 million plus), expensive to operate and with a very high fuel consumption. These vessels seldom carry capacity loads in terms of passengers but very large (up to 30 plus) live-onboard crews are retained even when passenger loadings are extremely light. Operating hours are limited by crew rest period regulations. This limits the extent to which these expensive capital assets (the ships) can be utilised. This very high-cost current manning arrangement is accentuated, in the case of CalMac, by unusually generous pay and conditions. It should further be borne in mind that under these conditions, each vessel requires two and a half crews, such that a 30-crew ship requires 75 seagoing personnel to operate it, a number which excludes associated shore-based personnel.

While such ships are costly to run, the service to and from many of the island and peninsular communities covered by them is of low frequency, with restricted operating hours and unhelpful schedules. Yet the cost to the public purse of subsidising these so-called 'lifeline' services is now far in excess of what can be regarded as value for money. It is a fact, and a shocking one, that every one of the routes run by David MacBrayne Group subsidiaries makes a loss and has to be subsidised (see Appendix 3).

As will be demonstrated later, the DMG has been unhealthily secretive about revealing its deficits on a route-by-route basis. It is possible, however, to extrapolate from what statistics are available, to estimate current losses by route and to translate these into subsidy per passenger (as shown in Appendix 3) and subsidy per island population (as in Appendix 4). The results are startling.

For five routes (Islay, Colonsay, Coll/Tiree, Barra/South Uist and the Small Isles) the subsidy is estimated at over £100 per round-trip passenger – well over that in some cases. For the Oban–Barra–Lochboisdale service, it is around £300 per round-trip passenger.

As for the annual subsidy per head of population, the Small Isles leads the field at no less than some £26,000 per man woman and child on those islands, or £100,000 for a family of four! Colonsay comes second at around £17,000. It is perhaps significant that in both these cases the vessels employed have such large passenger certificates that they could evacuate the entire populations of the islands served in a single trip with room to spare.

It should be stressed that these figures are estimates based on extrapolations, but are believed to be realistic as general orders of magnitude. It would of course be useful for more accurate values to be provided from official sources.

To understand how Scotland's state-subsidised ferry sector has fallen into this sorry financial mess, let us look at the forces that have been at work over time.

CHAPTER 2

EVOLUTION

Over the centuries, as people and goods were moved over significant distances, one of the fundamental questions was whether the sea could be regarded as a barrier or a highway. The answer lies in the technical and infrastructural conditions of the time. In fact the balance has alternated between sea and land travel over the centuries.

MUSCLE AND WIND

Until relatively recent historical times overland travel in Scotland, and in the Highlands in particular, was difficult, slow and dangerous. Much of the land was mountainous or covered by dense forest, intersected by firths and fast-flowing rivers. In terms of speed and load-carrying capacity, the coastal seaways offered huge advantages compared with travel by land, where the only practical options were feet or hoof over what were at best rudimentary tracks. For millennia, therefore, the sea was *the* highway.

The advantage of sea versus overland transport in pre-mechanised times may be understood by considering the carrying capacity of a horse. A packhorse can carry up to some 30 per cent of its body weight. Thus, a 1,000-pound (450kg) horse cannot carry more than 250 to 300 pounds (110 to 140kg) at, say, 2 or 3mph (3 to 5km/h). Where wheeled transport was feasible a cart with one horse and driver could move 1 ton at 3 or 4mph (5 or 6km/h). And of course range was limited. Horses and men needed periodic feeding and rest.

By comparison a 40-foot smack with a crew of three or four could transport 30 or 40 tons over virtually any distance at an average speed of, say, 4 to 6 knots (7 to 11km/h) if conditions were favourable.

Thus overland goods transport was in times past generally restricted either to strictly local trade or linking inland settlements with the nearest coastal creek or tidal river where sea transport could be accessed.

A further challenge of inland travel in times past was the need to cross innumerable firths, rivers, burns and bogs. Bridges were few until the nineteenth century, and in their absence the only alternative was fording or ferry, necessitating a further time and cost penalty. As early as AD 950 the Earl's Ferry, between Fife and North Berwick, was instituted to enable pilgrims to travel across the Firth of Forth to St Andrews and other holy sites.

There was one activity, however, that generated a demand for overland travel. That was the cattle droving trade. Cattle and other livestock have from time immemorial, and in many cultures, been a store of wealth and a tradable commodity. Droving cattle and other livestock to markets had been carried on in Scotland for many centuries. It was during the eighteenth and the first half of the nineteenth century, however, that droving peaked. The concept was simple. There was an overabundance of cattle in the Highlands, Islands and east of Scotland, and a ready and growing market in the south. Droves were assembled in the spring, often at local fairs or trysts. From thence the drove moved at the leisurely pace of ten or twelve miles per day to be sold at the big trysts of Crieff or Falkirk.

Cattle breeding was no less prolific on the Hebrides. To reach market, however, island cattle faced the obvious necessity of a sea crossing. The economic reality of this was neatly described by pioneer economist Adam Smith: 'Live cattle are, perhaps, the only commodity of which transportation is more expensive by sea than by land. By land they carry themselves to market. By sea, not only the cattle, but their food and their water too must be carried at no small expense and inconveniency.'

From this fundamental principle, where transport by sea is more expensive than by land, and where an open sea crossing is unavoidable as part of an overall journey, it is important to minimise the cost and hazard of shipment by selecting the shortest practical sea crossing. This is exactly what the drovers did. Where the droving routes crossed sheltered sounds, sea lochs or firths, cattle were swum across if the crossing was sufficiently smooth and narrow. There were many places where this was done, such as across the Kyles of Bute at Colintraive (Gaelic *Caol an t-Snaimh* – the swimming narrows).

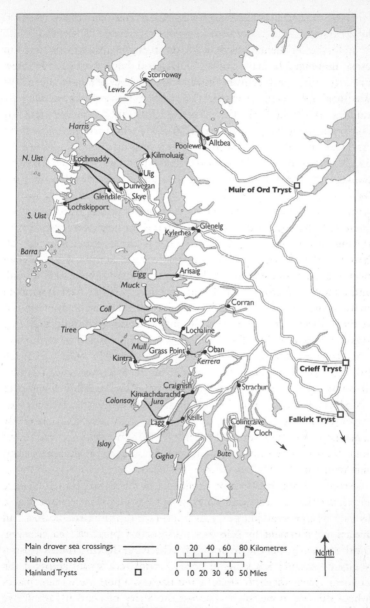

West Highland Drover Crossings

Droving aside, the sea remained the predominant mode for moving people and goods over long distances. The balance began to shift, however, from the mid-1700s with the creation of better roads. The turnpike system presented a solution, whereby tolls were levied to meet the cost of construction and maintenance. This enabled faster, more frequent, reliable and marginally more comfortable journeys by coach, and easier transport of agricultural produce and raw materials like limestone and coal by carters and carriers.

To help relieve destitution in the Highlands, the Commission for Highland Roads and Bridges was established in 1802 to undertake a separate programme of road, bridge and canal building with which the name Thomas Telford is indelibly linked.

Thus by around 1820, Scotland was crisscrossed by a network of metalled roads suitable for wheeled transport. The opportunities for overland travel for people and goods was revolutionised as was the development of postal services.

With the passing of the Post Office Act in 1711 the postal network expanded into Scotland's further-flung regions. By the early years of the nineteenth century most parts of the mainland had a regular postal service. Mail coaches ran between the main centres, the fastest averaging up to 10mph (16km/h). Smaller places were served by gigs, or rides, and the least populated areas by walks.

Prior to the middle of the eighteenth century, the conveyance of mails to and from the Isles was sporadic. In 1756 George Mackenzie, 'Steward and Receiver of Lewis', presented a request to the Postmasters General for a weekly packet boat from Stornoway to Poolewe and a foot runner from there to Inverness. This request was granted, and in 1758, representatives of the Uists sought a similar postal connection between Lochmaddy and Dunvegan. The onward overland link by a series of fords and ferries to Benbecula, South Uist and Barra remained a private responsibility until 1834.

In this way, the conveyance of posts to and from most of the Inner and Outer Hebrides and Orkney was handled by packet boats or ferries running to regular schedules between the islands and the nearest convenient mainland landing. These cross-water mail links largely followed the same short sea routes as the cattle trade.

STEAM

With the development of reliable steam navigation from the early nineteenth century, the balance shifted back to the sea. Travel by steamer was faster and cheaper than coach or waggon and more comfortable for passengers. An extensive network of long-distance passenger, mail and cargo steamer services from Glasgow, Greenock, Leith and Aberdeen expanded to serve Scotland's coastal and island communities.

Then a new faster mode of land transport – the railway – entered the scene. Little by little, the pattern of coastal shipping services would again be reoriented. Steamships were no longer the fastest means of transport.

In 1840 the Glasgow Paisley Kilmarnock & Ayr Railway (GPK&A) opened its main line and took over the Ardrossan Railway, thereby creating a direct rail link between Glasgow and the Ayrshire port. From that day to this, Ardrossan has been the favoured mainland port for Arran, cutting the time for the overall journey between Glasgow and Arran by roughly half as compared with 'all-the-way' steaming to and from Glasgow. In its new role as a railhead, Ardrossan also became a jumping-off point for Belfast and other ports.

The development of the railways in the Highlands came relatively late, but by the end of the nineteenth century they had reduced the prevalence of the long-distance sea routes by concentrating scheduled coastal passenger, mail and cargo shipping increasingly on railheads.

By the turn of the twentieth century the system of rail-connected steamer services was most intensively developed on the Firth of Clyde. The competing railway companies, equipped with their own fleets of fast, commodious saloon steamers, vied for the Clyde Coast trade, each operating from their respective railheads with fast train connections. These were the 'golden years' of the *belle époque* during which the Clyde resorts grew rapidly in population and rateable value. The two seasons 1906–07 marked the absolute zenith of Clyde services; 46 vessels (with a combined passenger capacity of 56,824) were in service on the Firth serving no fewer than 72 piers and 12 ferry landings. A nostalgic flavour of steamer travel at that time, viewed through the eyes of two small boys, can be gained from the first chapter of George Blake's book *The Firth of Clyde* in which a race between the GSWR Steamer *Mercury* and the 'Caley' *Duchess of Fife* is described in thrilling detail.

Although coal and labour were cheap, the competition was ruinous and by the mid-Edwardian period a measure of rationalisation was introduced. However the 'golden years' continued until the outbreak of the Great War. Steam navigation was approaching its peak of efficiency. Improved quality of steel boiler plates, and the higher steam pressures they afforded, led to the development of more economical compound and triple expansion engines. A further significant mechanical innovation in the period was the introduction in 1901 of the steam turbine. Offering fast, smooth, efficient operation, Clyde-built turbines were designed to give both long day cruises on the Firth and, in the form of fast liners and packets, to grace the world's short-sea and ocean trade routes.

The Firth of Forth was second only to the Clyde during this golden age, with intensive steamer services provided to 63 piers served by regular sailings or excursions. The River and Firth of Tay also had its fleet of steamers.

By 1912 David MacBrayne's legendary West Highland steamer fleet had reached its maximum size of 36 ships. In the east and north too, the service provided by the North of Scotland Orkney and Shetland Steam Navigation Company (colloquially known as the North Co.) had also reached hitherto unprecedented proportions, while the Orkney Steam Navigation Co. ran from Kirkwall to the Orkney North Isles.

Of course in those days, the smart Clyde railway paddle steamers, the turbines and MacBrayne's 'Royal Route' were the glamour – although predominantly seasonal – component of Scottish coastal shipping. The year-round business of moving people, mail and goods to and from our island and coastal communities was mainly in the hands of a much more economical and varied fleet of workaday craft. The pattern was characterised by two distinct styles of operation. One was the time-honoured unscheduled tramp point-to-point passage, undertaken, as demand required, usually with bulk cargo to a single destination. The other was the scheduled service, operating to a regular published timetable between mainland port or railhead, typically making a succession of calls en route to the final destination.

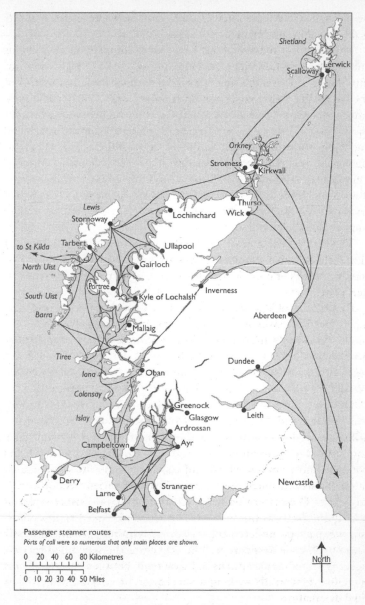

Edwardian Coastal Steamer Services

The outbreak of war in 1914 signalled the end of the halcyon days and Scotland's pre-eminence in maritime transport. Pleasure sailings were curtailed, and many celebrated steamers were requisitioned for war duty, a number never to return.

When the Great War was over, a kind of normality returned, but things were not as before. The steamship would prevail for many years, but great forces of change were underway. The economic situation had changed and steamer traffic never recovered its pre-war levels. Several services ceased altogether. The wartime shipbuilding boom was followed by slump. Too many effete sons and grandsons of the rugged enterprising men who had built up Scotland's maritime companies sold out to southern conglomerates. In 1923, the five big Scottish railway companies were 'grouped' under two huge London-controlled corporate bodies. Thus, within five years of the war's end, great swathes of Scottish wealth-creating capacity had been wrested from Scottish control. Key decisions would henceforth be made in London or Liverpool, not in Scotland.

INTERNAL COMBUSTION

A number of clever chaps in Europe and America were experimenting with alternatives to steam propulsion. The quest to develop a lightweight power plant to propel a horseless carriage culminated in the 1880s with the creation, by Gottleib Daimler and Karl Benz, of the first practical automobile. This employed the four-stroke internal combustion engine developed by Nicolaus August Otto. Whereas in the steam engine fuel is burned in a furnace within a boiler separate from the engine itself, the IC engine uses the explosive combustion of fuel within a cylinder to push a piston which in turn rotates a crankshaft.

By the dawn of the twentieth century, the motor car had arrived as a practical, if at first expensive, means of personal transport. With the introduction of the assembly line production sales soared, first in America then in Europe, and motor car ownership grew steadily.

It was not long before thoughts turned to marine applications. The first boat powered by a petrol engine was tested on the River Neckar in south-west Germany by Gottlieb Daimler and Wilhelm Maybach in 1886. They ran into opposition because irate locals had heard rumours that the boat was powered by explosions, which of course it was. Their fears turned out to be groundless and the trial was a success.

From 1905 a pioneering fleet of commercial motor vessels was assembled to aid the construction and operation of the hydroelectric plant and aluminium factory at Kinlochleven. There was no proper road to the site and supplies had to be brought in from Ballachulish by motor boat, provided firstly by local traders and later by David MacBrayne who introduced its own motor vessels *Comet* and *Scout*. *Scout* lasted only until 1913 when she was destroyed by fire after an engine blow-back. This set back further motor ship development for a time. The Kinlochleven service finally ceased in 1923 when the road was improved and motor bus and lorry services substituted.

The Advance of the Motor Vehicle

Petrol lorries and buses had appeared during the Edwardian period. It was the sale of cheap war-surplus lorries in the 1920s, however, that launched motor transport as a serious competitor to the railways and coastal shipping. They reached places not served by railways and increasingly competed with the railways and steamers directly, offering cheaper fares and a more frequent and flexible service.

One constraining factor in the 1920s was the poor quality of most of the road network, especially in the Highlands and Islands, where little improvement had been undertaken since Telford's day. Journey times by road were slow. Gradually throughout the twenties and thirties, however, significant improvement was made to the main road links by widening, improving alignments and macadamising surfaces.

After the Wall Street crash of 1929, the great Depression saw steamer passenger traffic slump. By the thirties, road transport had a competitive edge, such that the balance between sea and land transport was again shifting. On the islands from Arran to Shetland, private bus and haulage operators offered services that acted as feeders to steamer services, reducing the need for multi-port calls.

The case of Shetland is particularly interesting. The North Co. steamer *Earl of Zetland* operated an inter-island service from Lerwick twice a week to the North Isles and once a week to the north mainland ports – a time-consuming business owing to the lack of piers and the necessity for 'flit boats' to convey passengers and cargo between ship and shore. From the 1930s an island-hopping system known as the 'overland' was developed. Although north of Lerwick all the roads were single-track, the overland offered greater speed, frequency and convenience than the *Earl* for passengers, parcels and two-wheeled vehicles. It functioned as follows:

Bus from Lerwick to Mossbank (later Toft's Voe). Boat across Yell Sound to Ulsta on Yell. Bus from Ulsta to Mid Yell where all passengers and cargo switched to another bus. The second Yell bus ran from Mid Yell to Gutcher, then another boat across Blue Mull Sound to Belmont at the south end of Unst. From there another bus proceeded to Baltasound and other Unst communities.

The Shetland overland could not convey cars or other large vehicles. The few four-wheeled vehicles that were transported to the North Isles had to be derrick-lifted onto the *Earl of Zetland* and landed at one or other of the few piers or transferred perilously by flit boat.

Derrick-loading cars was almost universal on steamer services throughout Scotland prior to the advent of the car ferry. As an alternative, on the Firth of Clyde and a few other places, it was customary to drive cars and push luggage trolleys between pier and steamer across two stout planks at suitable states of the tide, a practice that continued until the 1960s.

On a number of short, sheltered water ferry crossings, from the early nineteenth century and possibly earlier in some cases, vehicles were similarly wheeled onto broad-beamed boats, athwartships, by the same expedient of planks linking boat with jetty. The first motor car was rowed across the Ballachulish ferry by this means in 1906 – a feat that was replicated on other short ferry crossings. In 1912, two motor ferryboats equipped with turntables were introduced on the passage to simplify the loading and discharge of cars. By the 1920s and 30s, to cope with the steady increase in car traffic, turntable ferries were in operation at Bonawe, Corran, Dornie, Glenelg, Kyle of Lochalsh, Strome, Kylesku and Kessock. From the occasional car in the first decade of the twentieth century, the Ballachulish ferry was carrying 42,000 cars annually by 1954 and 204,000 by 1974 when the ferry was replaced by the Ballachulish Bridge. The last turntable ferry still in operation – that between Glenelg and Kylerhea (Skye) – and nowadays something of a national institution, is operated without running subsidy by the locally owned Isle of Skye Ferry Community Interest Company.

There were far-sighted individuals in the inter-war years who saw a future in seagoing vehicle ferries on short crossings. One such was Dr Robert Forgan MP, who in 1930 asked the Secretary of State for Scotland what steps had been taken by the government to ascertain the practicability of a motor ferry between Dunoon and Cloch. The reply from the minister, Herbert Morrison, was less than visionary: 'I have been asked to reply. The proposal to establish a motor ferry between Dunoon and Cloch has not been brought to my notice by the local authorities concerned. I have ascertained, however, that the project has been discussed by the Dunoon Town Council and the railway company, but that it is not likely to mature.'

There was progress elsewhere. In 1929, the Dundee Harbour trustees built two new vehicle-carrying paddle ferry steamers for the Dundee–Newport Passage, to run on a half-hourly frequency. The service ended with the opening of the Tay Road Bridge in 1966.

On the Firth of Forth, historic Queensferry Passage between North and South Queensferry had been operated by the railway until 1934. In that year Maurice Denny, of the shipbuilding firm William Denny & Brothers, took over the operation. The Denny yard built two novel vehicle ferries for the route, each with capacity for 500 passengers and 28 cars. Such was the growth of vehicular traffic that two larger craft were added to the fleet. These conveyed 900,000 vehicles annually by the time they ceased operation in 1964 with the opening of the Forth Road Bridge.

New Motor Ships

As part of MacBrayne's post-1928 fleet modernisation, a series of new full-sized motor ships were built. The improvement in accommodation on the new ships as compared with the old was little short of revolutionary. Each ship had, for its size, spacious lounges, dining saloons and smoke rooms for two classes, together with comfortable state rooms for overnight travel.

From the operational point of view it had become clear that motor propulsion was economical. Coal and labour were no longer as cheap as they had been. Diesel machinery was much lighter than a steam plant and required no boiler. This freed up payload space. Nor did it require firemen to keep the furnaces fed. The main downside compared with near-silent steam propulsion, especially in the case of the earlier motor vessels, was noise and vibration.

In July 1939, a revolutionary new ship entered service under the LMS banner on the Stranraer–Larne route. She was *Princess Victoria*, the first railway-owned cross-channel motor ship and, more significantly, the first British purpose-built seagoing passenger and car ferry. Her main deck could take 80 cars, loaded over the stern via specially constructed link-spans at both ports. This innovation had become necessary because of the huge increase in demand for conveying cars between Scotland and Ireland. To get a measure of this traffic growth, as early as 1912, 120 cars were craned aboard the Stranraer service in August that year. Sadly the career of *Princess Victoria* was cut short by the Second World War. In May 1940 she struck a mine and sank with the loss of 34 of her crew.

Pioneer Aviators

One further application of the internal combustion engine was aviation, which was emerging as a practical transport mode in Scotland by the 1930s.

It is often forgotten that Scotland fostered many aviation pioneers. The earliest recorded was John Damien, who in 1507, equipped with feathered wings, leapt from Stirling Castle battlements in an attempt to fly to France. The attempt was unsuccessful.

The first successful ascent in Scotland was in 1784 at Edinburgh by James Tytler in a hot air balloon. In 1895 Percy Pilcher, a Glasgow naval architect, successfully flew in his bat glider near Cardross. Sadly as he was poised to fit an engine to an improved version in 1899, he was killed. Were it not for this accident, he may well have beaten the Wright Brothers to be first in achieving sustainable powered flight.

In the inter-war period a number of individuals were turning their attention to the idea of scheduled commercial passenger air services. Chief among them were Ernest Edmund Fresson in Inverness, Eric Leslie Gander-Dower in Aberdeen and John Sword based at Renfrew. By 1939, a network of Scottish air services had been created not dissimilar to that which exists today. It was not yet a major competitor to shipping services, but the future for aviation looked bright. Then with the outbreak of the Second World War, almost all civilian air services ceased with the exception of a few Irish Sea routes, Land's End to Scilly and Inverness to Orkney and Shetland. With those exceptions, the steamer and motor ship monopolised island transport links for the duration of the war.

THE SECOND WORLD WAR AND ITS AFTERMATH

Throughout the Second World War, many essential services were subject to travel restrictions as far as passengers were concerned or were suspended altogether.

Of the numerous Scottish coastal steamers called up for war service, in which many played a distinguished part, a significant proportion were never to return to home waters. With fleets reduced, a prevailing climate of austerity and higher costs, post-war coastal shipping services never resumed pre-war levels. The Firth of Clyde fleet, which had numbered 33 vessels in 1939, was reduced to 25 by 1947, and the number of Clyde piers used by passenger vessels likewise reduced from 53 to 34.

Three notable new ships appeared in that year. The first to materialise was *Princess Victoria*, on the Stranraer–Larne station. This was almost an exact replica of the previous short-lived but revolutionary stern-loading vehicle ferry of her namesake, which was lost in war service. The second was the new LNER paddle steamer *Waverley*, fortunately still sailing as the world's last seagoing paddle steamer. The third was *Loch Seaforth*, built for MacBrayne's Stornoway mail service.

As part of the policy of the post-war Labour government, the Transport Act of 1947 made provision for the nationalisation of the transport network. As a result of this Act, British Railways (BR) came into existence as the trading name of the Railway Executive of the British Transport Commission (BCT) and on 1 January 1948 the state-owned organisation took over the assets of the LMS and LNER, including those companies' steamers and port facilities.

Bringing the Clyde railway fleet under a single management allowed a measure of rationalisation. One such measure introduced on the railway fleet, but not other operators, was the abolition of the two-class system. Railway vessels sailed as one-class ships thereafter. Not long after nationalisation, the Railway Executive also started a process of increasing capacity on the Kyle–Kyleakin car ferry crossing.

Simultaneously with the nationalisation of the railways, the Glasgow–Hebrides service operated by McCallum Orme Steamers was absorbed by David MacBrayne Ltd, itself now partly nationalised on account of the former LMS's half share in the company. Some reorganisation of services to the West Highlands and Islands followed, and several cargo boat calls were replaced by road haulage to and from the next nearest port or by mail steamer. In 1949 the Islay mail service was extended to Colonsay to provide a more frequent service.

More radical change came on the back of a 1952 white paper which provided a subsidy to David MacBrayne Ltd of £360,000 per annum, subject to certain conditions, which included further substitution of road services for cargo ship calls.

In that same year Lord Hurcomb, Chairman of the BCT, announced a £1,000,000 plan to modernise Clyde services. This resulted in the building of seven new twin-screw motor ships, of which four were medium-sized passenger vessels for railway connections and short cruises (the *Maids*) and three side-loading vehicle ferries *Arran*, *Cowal* and *Bute* fitted with electric lifts or hoists to enable motor vehicles to be driven on and off at any state of the tide. This was an advance on former arrangements for carrying vehicles across the Firth, albeit a slow and cumbersome procedure. The rationale was that side loading with hoists permitted the use of existing piers, thereby obviating the need for the construction of link-spans and aligning structures.

The main duties of the vehicle ferries were shuttle services between Gourock and Dunoon, Wemyss Bay and Rothesay, and to Arran and Millport. These ships had a capacity for 24 cars or equivalent, later increased to 34 and, while noisy and utilitarian, they were much more fuel efficient than the traditional steamers they replaced.

In 1953 the Conservative government abolished the Railway Executive and control of BR was transferred directly to the BTC. Other changes included the return of road haulage to the private sector, while all the Firth of Clyde railway vessels were brought under the banner of the CSPCo (Caledonian Steam Packet Co. Ltd), originally a subsidiary of the Caledonian Railway.

A fourth and larger hoist-loading vehicle ferry, *Glen Sannox*, was added to the Clyde fleet in 1957 for the Arran run, and over the ensuing decade further small car ferries were built for the Kyle–Kyleakin passage.

Shipping Services outwith the State Sector

State ownership of coastal shipping extended only to those ships and services that had previously been owned (in whole or in part) by the former railway companies.

The Aberdeen-based North of Scotland Orkney and Shetland Steam Navigation Company Ltd remained steadfastly independent and set to the task of recreating a peacetime routine after serious wartime disruption. New motor ships were ordered and the pattern of sailings was broadly similar to that before the war, although sailings to Scalloway and the west Shetland ports and north Shetland Mainland ports were never resumed, being more readily served by bus and lorry from Lerwick. The new motor vessel *St Ola* took over the Stromness–Scrabster route, but now omitted calls at Scapa for Kirkwall. To reflect the switch from steam to internal combustion machinery, the words 'Steam Navigation' in the company title were changed to 'Shipping' in 1953.

While in former times the shipping service to Caithness could compete effectively with the circuitous and slow far north railway, it was no match for the efficient post-war door-to-door flexibility of road haulage, particularly after denationalisation. Calls at Wick and Thurso were abandoned in 1956. During the fifties, however, there was something of a boom in summer, mainly tourist, passenger traffic to the Northern Isles. In contrast, winter passenger numbers dwindled as daily air services provided an increasingly attractive alternative.

The Orkney Steam Navigation Company and Messrs Bremner served the Orkney North and South Isles respectively. South Ronaldsay and Burray were now linked to the Orkney Mainland by bus, lorry and car via the war-built Churchill Barriers, removing the need for a regular steamer connection.

Increasing Car Traffic

While the traditional operators of scheduled passenger and cargo services were struggling to retain revenue and to contain costs, operators of the little car ferries shuttling across the narrow sounds and lochs were experiencing a boom.

The urge by families to own a car and to tour the Highlands which had started to gain momentum pre-war, became unstoppable post-war. In ten years from 1951 to 1961, for example, vehicular traffic over the

Kyle–Kyleakin ferry had increased more than fourfold from 19,415 to 84,819.

In 1950, anticipating this trend, the Bute Ferry Company Ltd started a car ferry service across the Kyles of Bute on the old droving route between Colintraive (Cowal) and Rhubodach (Bute), using two landing craft working off the beach at either side of the passage. For the first time, motorists had easy and frequent access to and from the island without recourse to the expensive and precarious expedient of driving over planks on and off a steamer as dictated by tides. This project necessitated the construction of a road between the ferry landfall at Rhubodach and the Bute road network at Port Bannantyne; an investment that repaid itself many times over, bearing in mind the subsequent success of the vehicle ferry.

With the rapid growth of vehicle traffic on the short crossings, the inconvenience of queues at busy periods and the non-operation of ferries at night caused increasing frustration, it was inevitable that thought turned to bridging some of the water gaps to enable traffic to flow continuously. A number of such 'fixed links' were built and a list is given in Appendix 5.

While motor traffic on the roads and on the short 'smooth-water' car ferry crossings was increasing exponentially, many, if not all, of Scotland's traditional shipping services plying longer passages on more open waters were facing problems. Cheap and frequent bus and fast, frequent airline competition had eroded passenger traffic. Cargo operating costs rose, particularly because of cripplingly restrictive dock labour practices and the slow and laborious process of loading and discharging cargo by crane or derrick.

In 1961 the North of Scotland Orkney and Shetland Shipping Company Ltd was taken over by Coast Lines, so ending the company's independence.

The Orkney Steam Navigation Company was also faced with rising costs and with replacing their aging steamers, for which they did not have the financial reserves. In the west, patronage on the daily Portree mail ship service (Mallaig–Glenelg–Kyle–Raasay–Portree) had declined steeply because travellers to and from Skye were increasingly using the much more frequent Kyle–Kyleakin ferry either as foot passengers via rail–ferry–bus connections or in their own cars. The short, frequent Kyle car ferry and improving roads had clearly won the day.

To add to their woes, the traditional passenger/cargo/mail vessels were struggling to cope with the increased summer demand to carry cars, and in 1960, extra runs were provided on the Islay service during July and August. In that year too, the Highlands and Islands Shipping Services Act was passed. This authorised the Secretary of State to assist 'persons' concerned with the provision of sea transport services serving the Highlands and Islands under the terms of an 'undertaking' which was to be reviewed annually. The first beneficiaries of the Act were the inhabitants of the North Isles of Orkney. A new motor ship *Orcadia (III)* was built for the government and leased to a new Orkney Islands Shipping Company. She entered service in 1962. Compared with the old steamers, *Orcadia* was a great advance, with a comfortable observation lounge, cafeteria, bar and six two-berth staterooms. She was the first motor ship to serve the outer North Isles and as it transpired, the very last traditional derrick-loading passenger/cargo/mail vessel built for service in Scotland.

In 1987, Orkney Islands Council (OIC) assumed responsibility for the Orkney inter-island ferry services, and in 1995 Orkney Islands Shipping Company changed its name to Orkney Ferries Ltd. There are now 9 vessels in the fleet serving 13 off-islands, carrying over 82,000 vehicles and undertaking around 320,000 passenger journeys annually.

Also under the terms of the Act a new undertaking (i.e. contract) with David MacBrayne was announced in 1961 for a further ten years. In 1962 funding was approved for the building of three new vehicle ferries to operate between Oban, Craignure (Mull) and Lochaline (Morvern); Mallaig and Armadale (Skye); and a triangular route serving Uig (Skye), Tarbert (Harris) and Lochmaddy (North Uist). The ferries *Columba*, *Clansman* and *Hebrides* were built for the government and leased to the company at commercial rates, entering service in 1964. This was progress but, as hoist-equipped sideloaders, like the Clyde ferries, these vessels were by no means state of the art, bearing in mind that more efficient seagoing end-loading RO-RO ferries had been in operation in North America since before the First World War.

The introduction of the new one-class vehicle ferries led to the demise of the multi-port Sound of Mull and Outer Isles mail services and the class distinctions thereon. The comparative traffic figures for the Isle of Mull before and after the introduction of the vehicle ferry service demonstrates the impact:

	Passengers	Vehicles
1962 (traditional ship)	60,000	1,000
1970 (vehicle ferry)	250,000	27,000

NEW IDEAS

Around this time there was a flurry of research and report writing. In 1963 *Transport Services in the Highlands and Islands* noted that in the Highlands and Islands, airports, air, rail and many shipping and bus services were unremunerative, although the sea services to Orkney and Shetland provided by the North Company, the Aberdeen–Stornoway–Belfast–Liverpool cargo service provided by Coast Lines Ltd and tramp sea services all operated at that time without subsidy. It was also noted that road haulage had to quite a substantial extent replaced rail freight transport and operated without government assistance.

The report described how heavy cargo for the Inner and Outer Hebrides went by MacBrayne cargo ship at rates which were less than the combined cost of rail to west coast ports and onward shipment by mail ship to the islands. Nevertheless a third of MacBrayne's freight traffic went on the more frequent mail ship services. At that time, the only island with through mainland road haulage links was Skye, via the Kyle–Kyleakin ferry, which had captured much of the former sea cargo traffic.

The report opined presciently that the introduction of vehicle ferries to other islands could result ultimately in cargo services from Glasgow and Aberdeen being replaced by road and ferry services, and that Inverness, Dingwall, Fort William and Oban may all be in a better position to compete for the island trade. It was suggested that such a move would, on the one hand, increase the need for government assistance to cover annual charges, but on the other hand, development in new traffic and rationalisation of services would in time reduce the need for grants.

The report pointed out that the £260,000 annual grant to MacBrayne was paid on social grounds. The need for services and facilities to be progressively developed was stressed and it was stated that 'unless the

Highlands and Islands are provided with adequate modern transport they will fall further behind the rest of the country'. The report noted that improvement would involve radical change and recommended that a new permanent body should be set up to advise the government on Highland transport.

In 1961, while the ministerial report was in preparation, the Highland Panel recommended that charges to remote mainland centres should be used as a yardstick for determining sea service charges. This concept came to be known as the 'mainland comparison'. Pressure from the Panel in promoting this and other ideas, when added to the recommendation of the ministerial report once published, resulted in the government of the day setting up the Highland Transport Board.

The Highland Transport Board

The Highland Transport Board, chaired by R.H.W. Bruce, was appointed in December of 1963. In its 1967 report *Highland Transport Services*, it made a number of radical recommendations affecting all modes of transport in the Highlands and Islands. Bearing in mind the state of knowledge at the time, the content was of unusually high quality, offering new insights into how communities could better be served by more cost-effective sea transport.

The report noted some fundamental issues that would have a bearing on the future, including: the growth of passenger air transport as an alternative to travel by sea; the acute seasonality on the traditional passenger/cargo/mail ship services, and the emerging development of vehicle ferries.

An important concept stressed by the Board was the Norwegian experience of vehicle ferry operations and in particular that of the Norwegian fylke (county) of Møre og Romsdal, whose chief roads surveyor, Mr K.H. Oppegård, had recommended the adoption of simple Norwegian-style 'drive-through' vehicle ferries in Shetland (see below – 'Transformation in Shetland'). The aim of the Norwegian approach was to connect island and isolated mainland communities with the national road network by means of vehicle ferries operating on the shortest crossings utilising economical standardised vessels and terminals with minimum crewing. This resulted in low operating costs, high frequency and low fares, thus enabling them to perform as closely as possible the function of bridges.

The report then considered how these principles could be applied in the Highlands and Islands.

As far as Orkney and Shetland were concerned, all shipping links were then by traditional 'lift on/lift off' passenger/cargo or cargo ships. It was seen as doubtful that the North Company would be able to continue for long without financial assistance.

In terms of Orkney specifically, it was noted that in summer on the daily Scrabster–Stromness service the *St Ola* regularly loaded cars (by derrick) to capacity and had to be supplemented by the freighter *St Clement*. The Board's view was that a vehicle ferry service across the Pentland Firth appeared to be a future possibility.

The Board's deliberations on local Shetland services coincided with the then Zetland County Council's own investigations into transport options for the North Isles. The *Earl of Zetland (II)*, which performed a thrice-weekly round of the islands from Lerwick, was approaching the end of her life. The alternative daily overland route, which was operated by three different coach operators and two different boat operators, had captured much of the *Earl*'s passenger and parcels business, but could not convey vehicles.

The council concluded that a vehicle ferry system would be the best solution and invited the aforementioned Mr Oppegård to visit Shetland. He made a report advocating a system of vehicle ferries on a series of short crossings to replace the service by the *Earl of Zetland*. After further investigations, a system employing a series of short, frequent vehicle ferry crossings serving Whalsay, Yell, Unst and Fetlar was mooted.

In considering the best future pattern of shipping service for the Inner and Outer Hebrides, the Board were of the firm view that the future would lie largely with vehicle ferries of one type or another. The Board recognised, however, that the use of lifts, rather than the 'end-loading' roll-on/roll-off principle, with consequential delays in unloading, was not ideal. They suggested the introduction of the simpler and less expensive Norwegian-style vehicle ferries on routes such as Oban–Craignure–Lochaline and Mallaig–Armadale, and that pier modifications should be undertaken to suit these vessels.

Among a series of further recommendations for the Hebrides the most radical was that for Islay, Jura, Colonsay and Gigha.

Like the *Earl of Zetland (II)*, the Islay passenger/cargo/mail vessel

Lochiel was nearing her life's end. In time-honoured fashion *Lochiel* started each alternate morning either from Port Ellen (Islay) via Gigha, or from Colonsay via Port Askaig (Islay) and Craighouse (Jura), to West Loch Tarbert (Kintyre) where passenger and mail connection was made at nearby East Loch Tarbert with the Ardrishaig mail steamer for Gourock and the onward railway connection to Glasgow.

There were two rival schemes for replacing *Lochiel*. MacBraynes proposed a relatively large vehicle ferry operating between a new pier, to be sited in deeper water on the south side of West Loch Tarbert and Port Askaig (via Gigha and Craighouse), and onward to Colonsay (the Tarbert route). The alternative proposal (the overland route), supported by the Islay District Council and the Islay Transport Users Committee, favoured two or possibly three Norwegian-type ferries operating on the short crossing between Keills (Knapdale) and Lagg (Jura), thence by road through Jura to Feolin and a second short crossing of the Sound of Islay to Port Askaig and Colonsay. Gigha would be served separately by a small vehicle ferry running frequently between Tayinloan (Kintyre) and Ardminish (Gigha).

The Board strongly favoured the overland option on the grounds that, at up to ten round trips per day, it would give a much higher frequency of service, 'which has proved so important in attracting traffic', as compared with up to three round trips per day on the Tarbert route. Much greater capacity of 200 cars per day would be provided in each direction by a 20-car Norwegian ferry ($20 \times 10 = 200$) as compared with 120 cars per day in each direction by a 40-car capacity ferry via Tarbert ($40 \times 3 = 120$). The cost of building and operating the Norwegian-style vessels and terminals would be less than for the Tarbert route. The downside was the cost of upgrading the 17.37 miles and 10.97 miles of road on Jura and Knapdale respectively. The Board recommended that 'the cost of the necessary road works should be regarded as part of a comprehensive plan to improve sea and road transport approaches to Islay'.

The Board made a number of other recommendations, including cutting the number of long excursion sailings; abandonment altogether of the MacBrayne Ardrishaig mail service as soon as Tighnabruaich had improved road access; increasing capacity on the Kyle–Kyleakin ferry; replacing the open boats then in use between Fionnphort and Iona; a landing craft-type ferry or similar to be put in service on the short Port Appin–Lismore crossing in place of the service from Oban; and provision of regular vehicle ferry services using landing craft-type ferries between: Ludag (South Uist), Eriskay and Eoligarry (Barra); Castlebay (Barra) and Vatersay; Newton (North Uist), Berneray and Harris, and between Sconser (Skye) and Raasay.

As regards ferry terminals, it was recommended as possibly more economical to build new roll-on/roll-off terminals than to adapt existing piers, but that in general only one terminal per island could be justified other than where the island acted as a bridge, as recommended for Skye, Yell and Jura. Where traffic was significant, the Board opined that the additional cost of a specially designed Norwegian-style terminal with automatic locking device would generally be outweighed by the operating savings from the quicker turnaround of a roll-on/roll-off vehicle ferry of the Norwegian type.

The Board also noted that bridges or causeways had already created better transport links and suggested that there might be scope for further fixed links of this kind (Appendix 5).

At the termination of its period of office the Board had been reviewing the administrative provisions governing the regulation and control of ferries and made a number of observations concerned with the rationalisation of ferry planning, seeking more efficient investment choices and operational methods. There were a number of other details, observations and recommendations and all in all the Highland Transport Board's report was the most thoughtful, comprehensive and in many respects most radical ever published on sea services in the Highland and Islands.

The Highlands and Islands Development Board

The report was submitted to the newly appointed Highlands and Islands Development Board (HIDB), who considered it and, in its second annual report, paid tribute to the Board's 'excellent work', endorsing its conclusions.

In particular, the HIDB focussed on the high cost of freight, and the comparison with charges to remote parts of the mainland which 'showed great disadvantage suffered by island communities'. As an example, the report pointed out that on the mainland, freight could be transported on a heavy lorry for two old pence per ton mile, whereas freight shipped across the Minch ranged in cost from one shilling to four shillings per ton mile (between six and twenty-four times as much!). The HIDB made a special point of supporting the introduction of Norwegian-style ferries and ideas; the proposed overland route for Islay and Jura and that for the North Isles of Shetland; and a direct car ferry link between Stornoway and the north-west mainland.

Less than a year later the National Board for Prices and Incomes published a report examining the North Company's case for a proposed heavy increase in charges, reflecting a 20 per cent increase in dock labour costs due to dock labour decasualisation, resulting in reduced productivity, poor stowage and delayed cargo shipments. The question of future state subsidy was raised for consideration by the government.

The stage was set for the widespread introduction of seagoing roll-on/roll-off ferries along the lines set out by the Highland Transport Board. Sadly, with some important exceptions, the proven Norwegian principles were not adopted, resulting in decades of inefficiencies, less than optimum service and immense cost to the taxpayer.

Fares and Charges
On the vexed issue of fares and charges, the HIDB reiterated the High-land Panel's view and recommended that 'the general level of charges to islands should not be materially in excess of charges to distant parts of the mainland'. A detailed paper was prepared which described how a meaningful 'mainland comparison' might be realised, concluded that the simplest solution would be: 'To create conditions for transport to the islands which are truly comparable with those on the mainland. This means considering the appropriate ferry and shipping links as roads or bridges. The car ferry to an island and the piers are, in fact, parts of a flexible road over which cars and commercial vehicles can pass to and from islands.'

Until this time, cargo was charged according to a complex commodity scale based on tonnage or per item. The paper, which also recommended that a scale of linear charges on vehicles on RO-RO ferries should replace commodity charging, was submitted to the Scottish Development Department in 1968, and after four years of correspondence and discussion, the government's decision was announced in a parliamentary statement in 1972. The statement maintained the principle that charges levied on sea services should be based on operating costs (which they weren't), and agreed to the introduction of RO-RO ferries and to linear charging for vehicles. However it rejected the Norwegian concept that ferries should be regarded as part of the road system.

Road Equivalent Tariff

Concern about the burden of freight charges to island economies intensified and in 1974 the HIDB re-examined the issue. Case study analysis revealed that in many cases island business was indeed disadvantaged by sea freight charges. The then chairman of the STG, Sir Patrick Thomas, challenged the HIDB to explain how the concept of 'the mainland comparison' could possibly be made to work.

As a young transport research officer with HIDB, I was given the task in the two-week lead-up to Christmas that year of refining the case. This was duly set out in the report *Roads to the Isles – A Study of Sea Freight Charges in the Highlands and Islands*. In this document, the concept of 'Road Equivalent Tariff' or 'RET' was born.

The case as made is summarised as follows:

Payment of Road tax entitles road users to drive anywhere on the road system. Tax is used to construct and maintain roads. Roads go everywhere except for reasons of geography to islands (and a few remote peninsulas). Islanders pay road tax but are uniquely denied access to the great bulk of the road system without paying a substantial ferry surcharge. To be equitable, the cost to the road user of crossing the ferry ought to be related to the cost of travelling along an equivalent length of road. This would be achieved by charging a vehicle the equivalent of its road running costs. The shortfall between resultant revenue to the ferry operator and his costs would be met from taxation.

That was the logic. In preparing the report, I examined the operating costs of different types of vehicle and it became apparent that vehicle operating costs can be expressed on a mileage basis and related to the length of each type of vehicle. I found that the cost at that time was broadly around 2p per kilometre per metre of vehicle length. As an approximation of then current passenger fares, passengers were regarded as a one-metre vehicle for the purposes of calculating an appropriate fare.

I then created a formula to translate this concept into a linear ferry charge. The formula included a 'toll', equivalent to four kilometres of distance; these were similar to tolls charged to road users for exceptional capital expenditure. Thus a one-kilometre crossing would be charged as five kilometres, two kilometres as six, etc. The formula was set out as follows:

C. = L.O.D. + T. or L.O.D. + 4 L.O.

Where:

C. = charge for a single journey
O. = operating cost per kilometre per metre of vehicle length (average)
L. = length of vehicle in metres
D. = passage distance in kilometres
T. = toll element = 4 L.O.

In comparing the fares based on this formula with existing fares at that time, the general effect was that passenger fares remained broadly in line with those then obtaining, but RET vehicle rates were generally at a lower level those then in force, particularly for commercial vehicles, although not in all cases.

A criticism made by civil servants was that the application of a formula of this kind detached the charge levied for passage from an exact link with the operating cost of the vessel. With the charging regime then in force, there was in reality no such exact link.

As a counter argument, the analogy was made of the postal service which did not surcharge island letters and parcels despite the necessity for the cost of sea or air transport. The ship or aircraft operator is paid from general Post Office revenue for providing transport. Similarly under RET, it was proposed that the ferry operator would provide the road on an agency basis and would be paid for so doing from the roads budget.

In the event RET excited much interest but was ultimately rejected at that time by government on grounds of expense. It would be three and a half decades before its introduction by the SNP government.

As the original architect of RET, I have to say that my view is that it was of its time, but that communities and the taxpayer would nowadays be better served by more effective policy and operating methods, rather than blanket imposition of RET. My creation, like Frankenstein's monster, seems to have developed a wayward life of its own.

Debate and Development

The HIDB's 1975 *Highlands and Islands Transport Review*, which I also drafted, set out a raft of transport policies for the area with the aim of reducing economic disparity between the Highlands and Islands and the more affluent areas of the UK and the then EEC while having regard to the impact of development on the environment.

Among the numerous recommendations made were:

- Reiteration of the case for RET
- Designation of the Stornoway–Lochboisdale (spinal) road for special development
- As part of this: creation of a Berneray causeway and frequent ferries across the Sounds of Harris and Barra
- Upgrading of RO–RO ferry links with the mainland
- Improvements to mainland trunk road links, e.g. Tarbet–Ardlui
- Cessation of the Glasgow cargo boat service
- Multilingual presentation of information including Gaelic
- More visually attractive transport terminals

I was subsequently asked to draft a further HIDB consultative paper on ferries in 1978. This remained unpublished as I moved to other work, but it set out a more refined and detailed analysis of how the ferry system might be improved to the benefit of island economies in a cost-effective manner. In particular the concept of 'road equivalence' was expanded to ensuring that access by ferries comes as close as possible to that by road in terms of frequency, convenience and comfort, and not just fares.

It illustrated in practical terms how a radical restructuring of all Scottish ferry services could be achieved over the ensuing 20 years by setting out a programme developed from principles advocated by the Highland Transport Board. The main principles were:

- Adopt the shortest practical crossings
- Introduce economical Norwegian-style standardised vessels (general arrangement drawings were provided)

- Standardise link-spans along Norwegian lines
- Develop capacity through frequency rather than size of vessel
- Control costs (capital, crew, fuel consumption, etc.)
- Allocate routes to operators by means of competitive tender
- Allocate subsidies by route rather than by operator
- Require mandatory annual reporting of operating costs according to set standards

Fundamental to all of this was the 'shortest route' principle as a means of reducing fares, operating costs and the requirement for subsidy, while at the same time increasing frequency. To illustrate the point: if a 30-mile (two-hour) crossing can be replaced by a (one-hour) passage of 15 miles, a ferry would be able to make six round trips per day instead of three. It follows that to carry the same volume of traffic a ship of roughly half the size and therefore roughly half the operating costs is required. Where implemented, the effect of increased frequency coupled with reduced charges always generates new traffic and a requirement for increased capacity. The generation of new traffic is crucial for the growth of island economies.

Ten crossings in Scotland were identified as suitable for shortening at that time. These were:

- A Dunoon–Cloch shuttle
- Islay and Jura overland
- Loch Tuath (west Mull) to Coll and Tiree (Mull overland)
- Port Appin–Lismore vehicle ferry to replace Oban–Lismore
- Replacement of the 48km Uig (Skye)–Lochmaddy route with a 30km Glendale (Loch Pooltiel)–Lochmaddy route
- A Sound of Harris crossing
- A Sound of Barra crossing
- North Skye–Tarbert
- Caithness–South Ronaldsay (Orkney)
- Caithness–Shetland

The whole system was costed in terms of annualised capital costs of new standardised vessels, terminals, etc. and operating costs. If the programme suggested had been implemented, it was estimated that the savings on costs could have enabled the level of subsidy then budgeted for supporting ferries to reduce charges Scotland-wide to near RET levels. A sophisticated formula was devised to enable this to be done.

Unfortunately in the event, the opportunity was not taken by the government of the day to institute such a Scotland-wide programme. Where such methods were employed – in particular in Shetland and by Western Ferries on the Clyde, as will be demonstrated – traffic volumes have soared, to the benefit of those local economies, while subsidy costs per passenger or per vehicle have been much reduced or eliminated, to the benefit of the public purse.

ROLL-ON/ROLL-OFF

On an end-loading ferry, vehicles are driven on and off by means of a hinged ramp at either (or both) the bow or stern of the vessel which in turn engages with either a link-span or slipway. A drive-through ferry can load and discharge vehicles over both bow and stern by means of ramps on the vessel and link-spans. The advantage of these arrangements over the hoist-equipped side-loaders was ease of carrying full-sized commercial vehicles and rapidity of turnaround at terminals.

More than a century earlier, in 1850, the world's first seagoing end-loading RO-RO ferry came into operation. She was the *Leviathan* train ferry on the Firth of Forth. And there were of course cross-river, vehicle-carrying ferries introduced in the nineteenth century on the River Clyde and elsewhere.

As previously mentioned, the first seagoing stern-loading RO-RO, passenger/motor car ferry in British waters was the short lived Stranraer– Larne *Princess Victoria* of 1939. Her near-identical replacement, *Princess Victoria* of 1947, demonstrated the attraction of RO-RO to the motoring public and increasingly to hauliers. Tragically this fine vessel foundered in a severe storm in the North Channel in January 1953 with the loss of 133 lives. The main cause of this disaster was the design of the stern doors which were not of full height and which were breached by the mountainous seas experienced that day, allowing the vehicle deck to flood and swamp the ship.

This disaster undoubtedly caused a paralysis among the BTC top brass and for a time the Stranraer–Larne route was served by the aging conventional *Princess Margaret*, supplemented in summer by the Dover train ferry *Hampton Ferry* which dealt with the car traffic with the aid of planks laid over the rails on the train deck.

In 1960, the BTC-owned and renamed Caledonian Steam Packet (Irish Services) Ltd took over responsibility for the Stranraer services and in 1961 the stern-loading RO-RO ferry *Caledonian Princess* was launched and placed on the Larne station. Perhaps surprisingly for this late date, she was driven by steam turbines and was both a splendid vessel and a huge success. She could accommodate 100 cars and 70 cattle, 400 first- and 1,000 second-class passengers. Her success may be understood by her carryings of 46,000 vehicles and 300,000 passengers in 1963, yielding a profit of £370,000. Further rapid traffic growth necessitated more tonnage, culminating in the new larger vessel *Antrim Princess* – the first of a series of drive-through vessels built for the service.

The first to initiate the seagoing roll-on/roll-off technique in the West Highlands were Eilean Sea Services, who commissioned a new landing craft-type vessel, *Isle of Gigha*, in 1966 – just in time to take advantage of the seamen's strike of that year. She sailed mainly between Oban and several of the Inner Hebrides, clearly demonstrating the potential for a roll-on/roll-off ferry service. Tragedy struck, however, when she capsized that winter with the loss of two lives. *Isle of Gigha* was subsequently recovered and went on to have a long and successful career in West Highland waters.

Western Ferries Shows the Way

A new company, Western Ferries, was registered in 1967 with a more substantial capital base, to develop the RO-RO concept further. The company ordered a new vessel and started construction of a purpose-built terminal at Kennacraig in West Loch Tarbert (Argyll). As there was very little tidal range at this location, thereby removing the need for a link-span, the terminal was a relatively simple affair. The new ship, *Sound of Islay*, launched in February 1968, was a functional stern-loading ferry of Norwegian design capable of carrying 25 cars or 6 commercial vehicles and up to 75 passengers. *Sound of Islay* launched a new service to Port Askaig in Islay in April 1968 in opposition to the traditional David MacBrayne lift-on/lift-off mail ship *Lochiel*.

The new service was an immediate success. Two return crossings per day were offered and the famous island distilleries were quick to seize the opportunity of bringing in barley and exporting their distinctive peaty product by trailer rather than by the time-honoured but inefficient lift-on/lift-off alternative. Locals and tourists too were attracted by the simplicity and lower price of RO-RO service.

In *The Scots Magazine* of that August, Tom Weir was wholehearted in his praise of the new service and its positive effects on the island economy. He extolled the greater frequency of service and lower charges: half the price for taking a car on the route, compared with the MacBrayne service; diesel down by three old pence a gallon, and a flitting for £140 against the MacBrayne's estimate of £340. By then, the need for a larger vessel was clear and an order was accordingly placed with the Norwegian yard Hatto Verkstad.

The new vessel, named *Sound of Jura*, entered service in August 1969. She was of standard Norwegian design operated by six shore-based crew working in shifts and providing a carrying capacity of up to 250 passengers and 36 cars or 8 trailers. Her greater speed of 14 knots and fast turnaround at terminals meant three round trips per day were offered. That same year *Isle of Gigha* was purchased by Western Ferries, renamed *Sound of Gigha* and placed on a new shuttle service between Port Askaig and Jura, thereby offering Jura a thrice-daily mainland connection compared with the thrice-weekly offering by David Mac-Brayne. Clearly Western Ferries was mopping up.

To be fair to the old David MacBrayne company, it had been in nego-tiation since 1966 with the then Argyll County Council to institute a new RO-RO ferry on a somewhat shorter route to Islay and Colonsay from a new deeper terminal at Redhouse near the mouth of West Loch Tarbert. In anticipation of this new terminal, and in defiance of the Highland Transport Board's recommendation that the overland option was the preferable way of serving Islay and its neighbouring islands, a new purpose-built 47-car capacity ferry vessel *Iona (VII)* was ordered in 1968.

On delivery *Iona*, equipped for bow and stern loading, was the first drive-through vessel in the MacBrayne fleet. She was also equipped with a lift for side-loading at conventional piers. Then Argyll County Council backed out of its commitment to build the new terminal. Without the terminal the new ship could not operate the Islay service because she was too deep draught to use the existing West Loch Tarbert pier.

To resolve the matter, *Iona* was swapped for the CSPCo's shallower draft hoist-loading car ferry *Arran*, which was able to use the old pier. *Arran* may have been an improvement on the derrick-loading *Lochiel*, but she was no match for the smart, low-cost Western Ferries operation.

By the end of 1971 the then Secretary of State Gordon Campbell (Conservative) announced that, because of losses sustained by the Mac-Brayne service, he intended to withdraw subsidy for Islay and would leave Western Ferries as sole operators on the route.

The First Signs of Madness

Gordon Campbell changed his mind and the newly formed Caledonian MacBrayne (or CalMac, see below) stayed on the Islay route and ordered a new fast ship *Pioneer* to 'take on' Western Ferries. Extraordinary as it may seem, *Pioneer* required three and a half times the crew and about thrice the fuel for similar carrying capacity, or in the case of vehicles, less carrying capacity, than *Sound of Jura*. Only with a large, open-ended, guaranteed subsidy and predatory pricing was CalMac, with such an extravagant ship, able to 'compete' with Western Ferries – a blatant case of unfair subsidised competition.

Western Ferries' Managing Director, Andrew Wilson, pointed out, 'Given the same subsidy, Western Ferries would not need to charge at all'. It was later reported that CalMac were carrying MacBrayne haulage trailers back and forth empty on the route to make their traffic statistics appear less abysmal than they actually were.

Andrew Wilson called for sense to prevail in the interests of providing both high quality service and value for money. Was his well-argued case positively received by the government of the day? Sadly no. What followed was obfuscation, unworthy derision of Andrew Wilson's figures and unquestioning faith in Caledonian MacBrayne. What was debated behind closed doors in St Andrew's House, the Scottish Office's HQ in Edinburgh, will probably never be known. What is on record are debates in Westminster. These are very revealing of the government's biased attitude.

It was Lord Belhaven and Stenton, speaking in the House of Lords in June 1975, who set the ball rolling with the question to the new Labour government:

'Whether, taking account of representations from the people of Islay, they (the Government) will now allocate to Western Ferries a fair share of the £2½ million subsidy granted to Caledonian MacBrayne in view of the fact that Western Ferries are the principal carriers to the island.'

Several other peers joined in a similar vein with Lord Strathcona and

Mount Royal who felt that the public were entitled to know how much of the £2½ million subsidy was attributable to the Islay route.

It was Labour Minister Lord Hughes who responded on behalf of the government. He let it slip that the subsidy was actually about double the £2½ million figure on account of capital and other grants. He justified the lack of breakdown of losses on a route-by-route basis on highly specious grounds.

'If we did give a breakdown of these figures we would almost certainly have people whose routes were receiving a comparatively small subsidy, asking that the subsidy on their routes should be brought up the level of the higher ones and that, therefore, their rates should be reduced or vice versa.'

Lord Hughes then dismissed the figures produced by Western Ferries as 'propaganda'.

In August it was the turn of the House of Commons, where Bruce Millan, Minister of State in the Scottish Office, moved the approval of the subsidy arrangements for Caledonian MacBrayne.

On the matter of lack of route-by-route statistics, the Minister abrogated responsibility.

'The company (CalMac) has always taken the view that for a variety of reasons, including commercial reasons, it should not publish detailed losses on individual services. This is not the wish of the Government; it is a matter for the commercial judgement of the Scottish Transport Group. It is a practice which has neither been encouraged or discouraged by the Government.'

Opposition members (Conservative, Liberal and SNP) urged that the public were entitled to route information and that blanket subsidy was inequitable and counter-productive. The House was also reminded that Western Ferries had brought a better service, cheaper fares and lower operating costs. Their pleas went unheeded.

The Minister, unrepentant, concluded the debate.

'If we are to provide a decent service to the islands, it must be done by the nationalised concern because that concern has the obligation to run the service. This is not a doctrinaire attitude.'

Oh yes it is!

With a government majority, the motion was carried.

And so commenced a system of subsidisation without public accountability, which has continued to this day.

Fortunately Western Ferries found other fish to fry. For a time *Sound of Islay* was redeployed to open up a new route between Campbeltown, Kintyre and Red Bay in Northern Ireland. Then she was employed on lucrative contracts in connection with the oil industry. When these contracts dried up, *Sound of Islay* was sold in 1982 to Canadian owners. Another innovation was the introduction of *Highland Seabird*, Scotland's first fast (27-knot) catamaran passenger ferry. This Norwegian vessel of a type commonplace in Norway was tried on a number of passenger routes around the Clyde and West Highlands and for a time in the profitable business of transporting workers to the Kishorn fabrication yard. She also found intermittent employment in the Solent, Mersey and Irish Aran Islands, with mixed results. She was eventually sold in 1985 to Emeraude Lines of St Malo.

One venture above all was to secure the future of Western Ferries, and that stemmed from the purchase by the company of Hunter's Quay pier near Dunoon in 1969 and the opening of a new route between Inverclyde and Cowal (see below under 'The Battle for Cowal').

Meanwhile a series of organisational changes were underway in the state sector.

The Scottish Transport Group and Caledonian MacBrayne

Under the terms of the Transport Act 1968, the Caledonian Steam Packet Company Ltd was transferred to become a subsidiary of the government-owned Scottish Transport Group (STG), and in 1969 the STG purchased all of Coast Lines' shares in David MacBrayne Ltd thus gaining full control of that company.

From 1970, the profitable MacBrayne Bus Services were gradually carved up among the other STC bus-operating subsidiaries or abandoned, and the glorious red, cream and green livery faded from the scene.

To alleviate unacceptable queuing at the Kyle–Kyleakin ferries, two much larger double-ended 28-car ferries were ordered. These materialised as *Kyleakin* and *Lochalsh* which took up the station in 1971–72. Of the five ferries displaced, one went to Scalpay. The other four were converted to bow loading, two of which went to the Kyles of Bute service, taken over by the CSPCo in 1970, and two to serve on a new service on the short ten-minute crossing between Largs and a new slip at the Tattie Pier on Great Cumbrae.

Then the STG announced that it had acquired the share capital of Arran Piers Ltd. This enabled the company to begin conversion of the berthing facilities at Brodick and Ardrossan for end loading RO-RO operation. To operate the route the Swedish 50-car capacity, drive-through *Stena Baltica* was purchased and renamed *Caledonia (III)*, entering service on the Ardrossan–Brodick run in May 1970.

On that same day, MacBrayne's *Iona* commenced operation between Gourock and Dunoon under charter to the CSPCo. As this route had not been adapted for end-loading RO-RO operation, *Iona* operated as a side-loader by employing her hoist.

In 1971 the STG started a programme of ordering a series of eventually eight small bow-loading vehicle ferries capable of operating to slipways. These became known as the Small Island Class. They had a capacity for 5 or 6 cars and about 50 passengers. The first of these, *Kilbrannan*, opened up a new service between Claonaig (Kintyre) and Lochranza (Arran) in 1972.

In 1973, the Caledonian Steam Packet Company Ltd was amalgamated with the greater part of David MacBrayne Ltd to form Caledonian MacBrayne, commonly known as CalMac. The new company, as part of the STG, was given responsibility for most of the regular shipping services and cruises on the Firth of Clyde and the West Highlands and Islands. These services were to be operated on a commercial basis without subsidy, as were David MacBrayne Road Services, reconstituted as MacBrayne Haulage.

Although also part of the STG, a remnant of the old David MacBrayne Ltd remained to operate certain unviable services to be subsidised under the 1960 Highlands and Islands Shipping Services Act. These included the remaining cargo services, the Oban, Tobermory, Coll, Tiree, Barra and Lochboisdale service and that to the Small Isles. From 1983, all vessels were absorbed into the Caledonian MacBrayne fleet and David MacBrayne Limited became a dormant company.

From its formation, CalMac was committed to eventual conversion of most of its routes to roll-on/roll-off, and in that year a RO-RO Stornoway–Ullapool service was opened by *Iona*, replacing the traditional, much longer daily Stornoway–Kyle–Mallaig mail service. This was the first modern 'roll-through' service to be operated to the Outer Hebrides and as a consequence of the change, Stornoway benefited from a doubling of frequency to two return sailings daily (except Sundays). In due course *Iona* was replaced by a succession of larger vessels.

By 1975 CalMac had a fleet of four large drive-through and six stern- and side loaders, with link-spans at Ardrossan, Brodick, Gourock, Dunoon (side-loading), West Loch Tarbert, Port Ellen, Oban, Craignure, Lochboisdale, Ullapool and Stornoway. This was supplemented by no fewer than fourteen smaller RO-RO vessels operating to a variety of slipways. By these means Arran, Cumbrae, Bute, Islay, Jura, Gigha, Lismore, Mull, Morvern, Iona, the Uists, Skye, Raasay, Lewis and Harris and Scalpay were all accessible by end-loading RO-RO ferries – all in all a remarkable transformation within some five years.

A year later a purpose-built 17-car, 170-passenger double-ended ferry, *Isle of Cumbrae*, was introduced for the Largs–Cumbrae route and the last member of the David MacBrayne cargo fleet was withdrawn. Thereafter all freight handled by the company was moved by road and vehicle ferry.

Over the next quarter century, link-spans at ports served by CalMac were installed at Wemyss Bay, Rothesay (side-loading), Uig (north Skye), Tarbert (Harris), Lochmaddy (North Uist), Mallaig, Armadale (south Skye), Coll, Tiree, Barra and Colonsay. Slipways were provided with aligning structures and new slipways created on each of the Small Isles of Eigg, Muck, Rum and Canna.

Over those years up until the turn of the millennium, new vessels were commissioned more or less on an annual basis to replace older vessels. The company abandoned cruising on the Firth of Clyde. The Kyle–Kyleakin route ceased with the opening of the Skye Bridge in 1995. On the other hand two important new services were inaugurated across the Sounds of Harris and Barra creating the long-desired Outer Hebridean north-south 'spinal route'.

Transformation in Shetland

After its fruitful exchanges with Norway, the Zetland County Council, as it then was, ordered five new ferries each with a capacity of 10 cars and 93 passengers to serve the Shetland North Isles. They were of a type very similar to vessels being used in Norway at that time. An extensive programme of pier and link-span construction, again on the Norwegian model, was also undertaken. The new vessels entered service sequentially between 1973 and 1975.

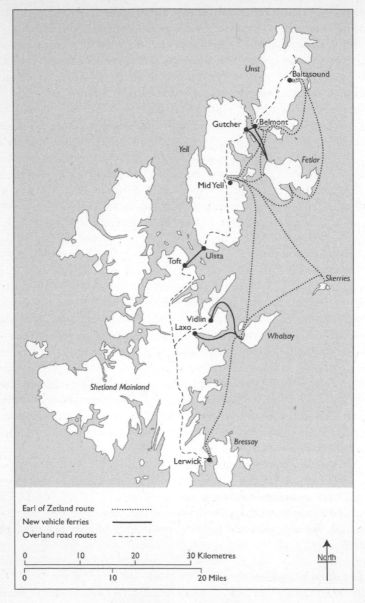

Shetland Ferry Revolution

As in Norway, vehicle ferries run for 18 hours per day and it has been the policy of the council to set fares and charges at a very low (less than RET) level to encourage usage. The new ferries proved even more popular than predicted and usage increased rapidly. Their success may be judged by the following figures which give a sense of the enormous growth in traffic since the last days of the *Earl of Zetland*.

Year	Passengers	Vehicles
1965 *Earl of Zetland*	20,000	173
Vehicle Ferries		
Original estimate in 1961	42,700	14,150
1976	178,000	75,000
2012	750,000	350,000

It soon became apparent that the original ferries were too small to cope with traffic on the busier routes. This necessitated augmentation by larger vessels over the ensuing three and a half decades. These services are funded by a combination of revenue receipts and subsidy from the Shetland Islands Council (SIC).

SIC currently own and operate a fleet of 12 ferries providing services entirely within the Shetland archipelago. The services run from 16 terminals serving 9 islands with a total population of just under 3,500 people. Freight and limited passenger services operate to Skerries, Fair Isle, Foula and Papa Stour.

There is absolutely no doubt that the Shetlanders' adoption of short, frequent ferry crossings on the Norwegian model has paid enormous dividends in maintaining the economies and social well-being of the inhabitants of the outlying islands of the 'Auld Rock'. The SIC is now considering the possibility of replacing some ferry crossings by fixed links.

The Battle for Cowal

In 1971, Western Ferries was in negotiation with Dunoon Town Council to open up a RO-RO service from Dunoon in place of the CSPCo's hoist-loading service to Gourock but, on the casting vote of the provost, the CSPCo retained the privilege. Then the decidedly odd decision was made to equip Dunoon Pier with a link-span at right angles to the face of the pier, interfacing with *side* ramps on new vessels to be designed for the route and so slowing the loading of vehicles, particularly large commercials.

This blunder was sufficient to encourage Western Ferries to operate its own drive-through service from its own terminal at Hunter's Quay on the shorter crossing to McInroy's Point, on the outskirts of Gourock.

In the spring of 1972 work started to create *end*-loading facilities at both terminals. That same year, two second-hand double-ended Swedish ferries were purchased. The first was *Olandssund IV* with a carrying capacity for 25 cars and 200 passengers. In 1973, after delivery from Sweden, extensive overhaul and renaming as *Sound of Shuna*, she started plying the route, giving an hourly service from 07.00 from Hunter's Quay to 23.30 from McInroy's Point. The one-way fare was £1 for a car and 25p for a passenger. Caledonian MacBrayne, the successors of CSPCo, immediately reduced their fares on their parallel route. A month later the second, slightly smaller Swedish ferry *Olandssund III*, started to provide an enhanced half-hourly service at weekends. She was renamed *Sound of Scarba*. In the six months to the end of the year Western Ferries had secured 34 per cent of cars moving between Inverclyde and Cowal. The competing CalMac service was worked by *Glen Sannox* and *Maid of Cumbrae*. Whereas the Western Ferries' vessels each had a crew of four, the *Glen Sannox* had a crew of no fewer than 27.

By summer 1974 traffic on Western Ferries' Clyde–Argyll ferry service had grown to such an extent that a half-hourly service was now required daily at morning and evening peaks and a midnight service was also provided. A third, second-hand ex-Isle of Wight ferry, *Lymington*, was purchased that year and she entered service as *Sound of Sanda*. Other vessels were added to the fleet in ensuing years.

In 1974 too, the newly formed CalMac placed its new 38-car, side-loading, so-called, 'streakers' *Juno* and *Jupiter* (each with a crew of ten) on their longer but adjacent Dunoon–Gourock route on a half-hourly frequency. Nevertheless, by the early 1980s, the frequent and profit-able unsubsidised Western Ferries operation, with its second-hand but simple, efficient and economical vessels, had captured some 70 per cent of the car traffic, notwithstanding subsidised competition from the new, custom-made but fuel-hungry CalMac ships. In 1982, after protracted negotiations, the Scottish Office decided that CalMac could continue operation between Dunoon and Gourock, but restricted to hourly frequency and that only the passenger element would be subsidised. In fact there was no attempt to separate the subsidy as between cars and passengers.

By the early years of the twenty-first century, Western Ferries had captured about 90 per cent of the Cowal vehicular traffic and two thirds of the passenger traffic, utilising four up-to-date economical vessels, giving a 15-minute frequency a peak times with operation to midnight at weekends. The company provides a 24-hour call-out service for ambulances carrying emergency cases – a quality of service unknown elsewhere in Scotland. In 2007 the car-marshalling areas were enlarged and second link-spans at both Hunter's Quay and McInroy's Point were installed.

Bearing in mind the superior level of service provided by Western Ferries at no cost to the public purse, it was difficult to justify the subsidised CalMac vehicle ferry service where, latterly, average carryings were around eight vehicles per crossing. With the restructuring of CalMac in 2006, their Dunoon service was transferred to Cowal Ferries, another DMG subsidiary. Towards the end of 2009, the European Commission issued its decision on the question of subsidies to CalMac/Cowal Ferries. The report considered the issues in some depth and it was essentially a legal ruling, which stated that the state aid granted to Cowal Ferries for the passenger element of their operation of the Gourock–Dunoon route was incompatible with Article 86(2) of the Treaty, and that CalMac had failed to ensure that there was no cross-subsidisation of vehicular traffic guarantees in place. It was then discovered that Cowal Ferries had been carrying commercial vehicles at well below cost.

It was, however, further stated that a new open, transparent and non-discriminatory public tender for a passenger-only public service contract would be acceptable. In that circumstance, the Gourock–Dunoon vehicle ferry service was not included in the next tendering of CalMac routes. In 2011, a £10.6m contract was confirmed between the Scottish Government and Argyll Ferries (a new David MacBrayne subsidiary) to maintain a passenger-only connection between Dunoon and the Gourock railhead as a public transport operation. To put that into perspective, an official report of 2007 noted that at that time only one in ten passengers on the route made a rail connection.

As in the case of Shetland's inter-island ferries, the short, frequent Western Ferries crossing by economical vessels proved to be the winning formula.

The Pentland Firth

The Highland Transport Board had noted a widespread public scepticism in Orkney about the idea of roll-on/roll-off vehicle ferries. Yet, while the numbers of passengers carried on the long route between Leith, Aberdeen and Orkney had collapsed in the face of airline competition, the slow derrick-loading methods were struggling to cope with the large number of cars presented for shipment between Scrabster and Stromness.

In recognition of this, the Board believed that a vehicle ferry across the Pentland Firth was feasible and that: 'if the shortest route across the firth were chosen, a vehicle ferry could make two or three return trips per day, and given a reasonable load factor, this could keep sea transport costs down.' To advance the idea they recommended that a Pentland Firth vehicle ferry crossing should be the subject of a comprehensive study.

The study carried out by HIDB considered two rival options. These were the existing Stromness–Scrabster route and a short crossing between South Ronaldsay (connected to the Orkney Mainland by the Churchill Barriers since 1945) and the nearest Caithness landfall. Regrettably the study ignored the short crossing's advantages of frequency and lower cost and plumped for the much longer Scrabster–Stromness route in the mistaken belief that the sea conditions in the eastern firth were unsuitable for a vehicle ferry operation – a serious misjudgement.

The die was cast. A new RO-RO ferry, *St Ola (III)*, with a capacity for 90 cars and 400 passengers, commenced operations for the North Company in 1975. It was in 1975 too that Coast Lines was taken over by P&O and the traditional North of Scotland Orkney & Shetland Shipping Company name ceased to be used. In the following year the number of cars shipped across the Pentland Firth rose to 15,000 as compared with 9,500 in the previous year. Mysteriously, the widespread public scepticism about RO-RO ferries evaporated. *St Ola (III)* provided only one return trip daily on the two-hour crossing as compared with the two or three return trips suggested for the South Ronaldsay short sea route.

In 1992 a larger (but older, German-built and second-hand) replacement Pentland Firth ferry was acquired and given the name *St Ola (IV)*. P&O Scottish Ferries also operated the long Aberdeen to Orkney and Shetland routes which by this time had also become RO-RO operations subsidised by the government.

Meanwhile, the idea of the short crossing had not been forgotten. A number of individuals had a go. In the summers of 1972 and '73 Captain William (Bill) Banks operated a summer twice-daily passenger run between St Margaret's Hope and John O'Groats with a converted 75-foot air-sea rescue launch he named *Pentalina*, carrying 12,000 passengers in the first season. Next came Ian Thomas and Donnie Bews who started with a water taxi service across the Firth and then, from 1976, a summer-scheduled passenger service on the very shortest 40-minute crossing between Burwick at the southernmost point on South Ronaldsay and John O'Groats. This John O'Groats ferry service continues to this day with *Pentland Venture* offering between two and four return trips daily, connecting with coaches between Inverness and John O'Groats and an extensive range of bus tours of Orkney. This service does not, however, carry vehicles.

It was Andrew Banks, nephew of Bill Banks, who in the end, and in the face of a sustained campaign by the powers that be to undermine his efforts, created the vehicle-carrying short crossing between Caithness and South Ronaldsay more or less as had been recommended by the Highland Transport Board. The story is set out in detail in my book *Pentland Hero*, but in a nutshell, with a tiny team of trusted colleagues and without a penny of public money, Andrew Banks built terminals at Gills Bay, near John O'Groats (Caithness) and St Margaret's Hope in South Ronaldsay. OIC refused to give him access to Burwick and the shortest feasible crossing.

In 2001, with the ex-CalMac ferry *Iona*, now renamed *Pentalina B*, his company Pentland Ferries commenced operations with a thrice-daily service between the two terminals. This was a hitherto unprecedented quality of access that allowed Orcadians to spend either four or eight hours on the Scottish mainland and return within the same day. At first the service was seasonal, and it was extended and supplemented after a couple of years by a second ex-CalMac ferry *Claymore*.

Tendering Shambles

In 1995, in response to the requirements of European law, the then Scottish Office announced that future subsidies for shipping services would have to go out to tender. The first contract to be put out to tender under the new arrangements was that for the three Northern Isles routes in 1997. In the event, P&O, the incumbent operator, was awarded a five-year contract covered by an annual block grant of £11 million. This five-year contract was, however, presented as a holding operation pending a new tender to operate from 2002 that would follow a re-evaluation of Northern Isles services.

The next Northern Isles tender process commenced in 1998 when the Scottish Office advertised for expressions of interest by potential operators. NorthLink Orkney and Shetland Ferries – a 50-50 partnership between Caledonian MacBrayne and the Royal Bank of Scotland to be known as NorthLink – were pronounced winner. New fast ships *Hjaltland*, *Hrossey* and *Hamnavoe* costing £30 million apiece, extra sailings and fares lower than P&O's were to be provided for an annual subsidy of £10.8 million in the first year, reducing to £7.8 million in the fifth. It seemed too good to be true. It was!

Meanwhile in 2000 it was announced by the new Scottish Executive that the Caledonian MacBrayne routes would be tendered and a consultation document published. Among the issues debated were: the setting up of a separate vessel-owning company and whether CalMac's routes should be franchised individually or as bundles or as a single franchise. The single franchise option was strongly lobbied for by CalMac and others on the grounds that it would deter 'cherry-pickers' only interested in the profitable routes, leaving CalMac with those that were unprofitable. What this oft quoted, but erroneous proposition failed to recognise was that not one CalMac route was profitable. There are *no cherries*. In fact the most attractive routes to a contractor may well be those low-volume routes that attract a high per-passenger subsidy.

In the event the then Scottish Executive opted to tender all the CalMac routes as a single package, with the exception of Gourock–Dunoon, which was to be tendered separately as Western Ferries legitimately objected to unfair subsidised competition. The upshot was the formation in 2006 of the vessel-owning company Caledonian Maritime Assets Ltd (CMAL) to lease ships to the winning operator, who was obliged to operate these ships on the same routes to the same timetables and charging the same fares, and to employ all the existing seagoing staff on the same pay and conditions. This meant there was no scope at all for innovation.

It was not until 2006 that the complex tendering process actually started. Of the interested bidders, only three were serious contenders. Two of those withdrew due to the complexity and expense of the tendering process, leaving CalMac, whose costs were met by the public purse, as the only contender. There were no bidders for the Gourock–Dunoon route which was to operate without subsidy. Eventually towards the end of 2007 a restructured Caledonian MacBrayne Ferries was awarded a six-year contract to run the Clyde and Hebridean ferry services, with the new Caledonian Maritime Assets Ltd owning and leasing out the vessels and the terminals formerly owned by CalMac. The whole process had cost the Scottish Executive well over £15 million in restructuring, civil service expenses, legal and other costs.

Much was made of the ability of ships within the CalMac fleet to be switched from route to route to cover periods of annual overhaul or breakdown. This is not unique to CalMac. Worldwide, most operators manage this without much fuss or difficulty. In fact the CalMac/ CMAL fleet is composed primarily of two distinct types of vessel, terminal and mode of operation. Between these there is virtually no interface. Thus the 'small' ferries operating with shore-based crews to slipways with no pre-booking facility are a wholly different type of operation from the Class IIA (European Class B) vessels. At the very least, the small ferry and Class IIA routes could have been treated as two separate bundles.

Back on the Northern Isles, the NorthLink contract had not performed well. In fact it had become clear to the NorthLink management that the budget on which their tender had been based had been completely unrealistic. The whole operation was losing money and the company was about to go bust! There were lame excuses, but a further £63 million was thrown at NorthLink to keep the show on the road pending early re-tendering.

In 2005 a short leet of three shipping companies were to be invited to bid for the Northern Isles ferry services, one of which was Caledonian MacBrayne Ltd. The Royal Bank of Scotland would own the ships, which the winning contractor would be required to operate. Bearing in mind that other bidders had been excluded on grounds of poor financial performance, the inclusion of the financially inept Caledonian MacBrayne as a potential contractor astonished many.

In 2006, despite this inconsistency, a six-year contract for ferry services to Orkney and Shetland was awarded to none other than NorthLink Ferries Ltd, the company now a wholly owned subsidiary of Caledonian MacBrayne. The budgeted subsidy for the first year of operation was set at an unbelievable £31 million – a far cry from the £7.8 million originally budgeted. This sum would be subject to adjustment as necessary in the light of actual inflation and other factors – a blank cheque, to all intents and purposes!

And so, to quote from *Pentland Hero*: 'after the rigmarole of re-tendering, the company, essentially unchanged, that had so seriously misjudged its market, so extravagantly designed its ships, so avariciously consumed vast amounts of public funds, had been favoured by an inept Scottish Executive administration with a further six years and an even vaster level of annual subsidy.'

On the Firth of Clyde, Cowal Ferries, another subsidiary of the David MacBrayne Group, continued to operate the Gourock–Dunoon vehicle ferry, subsidised ostensibly only in terms of its passenger service. Such was the disquiet about the process by which the subsidiaries of the David MacBrayne Group were funded that a European Commission investigation was launched in 2008, and in its 2009 report it concluded that while the arrangements were broadly compatible with state aid rules, the Gourock–Dunoon route should be opened to a transparent and non-discriminatory tender. Such was the delay in fulfilling this obligation that it wasn't until 2011 that of the four bidding concerns, Argyll Ferries Ltd, a new subsidiary of the David MacBrayne Group, won the tender to operate the route as a two-vessel, passenger-only service.

While these deliberations were under way, time was running out for the 2006 Northern Isles contract.

With public money being thrown at NorthLink, Pentland Ferries' business grew without any public subvention whatsoever. Andrew Banks was sufficiently encouraged that he ordered the building of a new, efficient, environmentally-friendly catamaran *Pentalina* from the FBMA yard at Cebu in the Philippines.

Once in operation from 2009, *Pentalina* was a winner. In that year, and each subsequent year, carryings increased exponentially, such that in summer the ship is now operating at capacity. It is clear that the additional traffic generated by Pentland Ferries has helped enhance the Orkney tourism economy at a time of economic recession.

In anticipation of the next Northern Isles tender, Andrew Banks, proprietor of Pentland Ferries, wrote to successive transport ministers suggesting a better deal for Orkney ferry users and offering the Scottish Government a realistic way of greatly reducing the spiralling public funding for ferry services to Orkney.

In doing so he updated the ministers on the reliable performance of the then new *Pentalina* on the Gills Bay (Caithness)–St Margaret's Hope (Orkney) route and the significant traffic growth, achieved without any need for public funds. He pointed out that Pentland Ferries provided the shortest, cheapest, most frequent and fastest-growing year-round service for passengers, cars and freight across the Pentland Firth. At that time 38.6 per cent growth in passengers and 61.5 per cent growth in cars had been achieved since *Pentalina* had been introduced. In contrast, notwithstanding receipt of massive subsidies, traffic on the parallel Stromness–Scrabster route operated by NorthLink was declining, the reason being Pentland Ferries' competitive advantage of shorter route and much more cost-effective technology and operating methods. In a nutshell he offered a better service for around a quarter of the operating cost of NorthLink's operation.

He reiterated the mantra of the short crossing, that the Pentland Firth ferry crossing is in effect a bridge between Orkney and the Scottish mainland and that few passengers or vehicles originate at, or are destined for, the port at either end of the passage. He contended, therefore, that most traffic was involved in longer transits, in which case the choice of the terminal ports should be determined by operational advantage, not historical accident. In this context he offered the Scottish Government a deal to create a much-enhanced ferry service across the Pentland Firth while simultaneously offering inducement to Orkney Islands Council (OIC) to replace aging vessels on their North and South Isles ferry networks – all at significantly reduced cost to the public purse. The main components of the arrangement were:

1. The Pentland Firth crossing would be separately tendered and the terminal ports left unspecified.
2. Pentland Ferries would bid for the service asking for an annual subsidy of circa £2 million per year for five years (compared with

an estimated annual subsidy of some £10 million for NorthLink Pentland Firth service).

3. Pentland Ferries would build a second new and improved *Pentalina* to provide increased frequency in summer, cover for winter overhaul and availability for charter elsewhere on the Scottish ferry network.

4. Pentland Ferries would guarantee fares at around current levels, adjusted for inflation, at least five or six return crossings daily in the peak summer period, at least four daily sailings in the shoulder period and at least three daily sailings in winter.

5. He further suggested that £2 million per annum be allocated for five years to kick-start a ferry-replacement programme on the basis that the OIC match this with funds from their Oil Disturbance Fund

After five years the subsidy regime could cease unless some future development or other arrangement were envisaged.

This was a win-win scenario. The Scottish Government would save up to some £6 million per year in the medium term and £10 million per year thereafter. Orkney would receive a high-frequency, near 'road-equivalent' ferry access, thereby stimulating economic development on both sides of the Firth. OIC would be compensated for loss of revenue and would be aided to embark on a ferry-replacement programme.

Andrew Banks signalled his ambition to operate between Gills Bay and the nearest Orkney landfall of Burwick to enable an even shorter crossing and higher frequency of service than is possible with the current Orkney base at St Margaret's Hope. He ended by confessing that under past Scottish administrations Pentland Ferries had felt at best sidelined and at worst undermined and suggested that his proposal was an opportunity for the current Scottish Government to recognise the success of this pioneering enterprise and its potential to provide a better and more economical ferry service for Orkney.

In due course the tender was launched; its specification being essentially the status quo but with additional Aberdeen freight runs.

Those of a cynical bent, and in this instance I include myself, believed it would be another shoe-in for David MacBrayne Group subsidiary NorthLink. It came as something of a surprise that when the winner of the tender for the new £242 million contract (that is

£40.3 million annually) to provide the Northern Isles ferry services as from 2012 was announced as the international service company, Serco Group PLC (Serco).

It was not Serco's fault that it had inherited a 'turkey' in terms of wasteful ships and in the case of the Pentland Firth a hopelessly uneconomic route. It was no surprise that within a few months of winning the tender, the company announced that it planned to reduce winter frequency on the Scrabster–Stromness route and to downsise the workforce. There was much consternation and political posturing in spring 2013 when *Hamnavoe* was pulled out of service for a month because of a broken crankshaft. In the event Pentland Ferries coped well with all the traffic on offer.

In fact by 2012, Pentland Ferries had already overtaken NorthLink in the number of cars shipped over the Pentland Firth and indeed in passengers too, when combined with John O'Groats Ferries, the other unsubsidised private operator on the Firth.

The Lessons from History

In comparison with land travel, the sea has in times past offered a cheaper and faster means of moving people and goods. At other times, it has been an expensive barrier. Nowadays road transport is so efficient and prevalent that scheduled coastal sea transport is, for the most part, no longer competitive unless it bridges gaps in the road network where sea intervenes, such as access to and from islands or remote peninsulas.

A number of independent vehicle ferry operators have demonstrated that it is possible to provide efficient and frequent services at modest cost to the travelling public and at no cost to the taxpayer. In contrast the state-owned or controlled sector has fallen into a dependency on vast amounts of annual subsidy while often providing an indifferent service. To find out why, it is necessary to look at the sector's approach to vessel design, capital costs, fuel consumption, crewing costs and operating methods

CHAPTER 3

THE HIGH COST OF THE
PUBLIC SECTOR

SHIP SHAPES

There are few parts of the world that Alf Baird hasn't visited in the course of his maritime researches as Professor of Maritime Business at the Transport Research Institute (TRI) at Edinburgh Napier University. The list of shipping companies, container terminals and ferry operations he has advised is a long one; perhaps longer than he himself can now recall. His international reputation on such maritime matters is second to none.

He makes the point that Scotland is unusual in the high proportion of its ferries owned and operated by public sector providers, whether local authorities or state-owned companies. As we have seen, the big players in the Scottish state-owned ferry scene are Caledonian Marine Assets (CMAL), which owns ferries and terminals, and the David MacBrayne Group and its subsidiary Caledonian MacBrayne Ferries, which operates ferries leased from CMAL.

Professor Baird demonstrates that, in comparison with the private sector, the state-owned ferries perform not just marginally badly but conspicuously so in terms of capital cost, crewing and fuel consumption, such that huge subsidies are required to prop up their inefficient operation. Yet they still lose market share to much more competent unsubsidised private operators, such as Western Ferries and Pentland Ferries.

The following table, for example, illustrates the huge difference in the cost of providing the two competing services between Orkney and Caithness.

Pentland Ferries and NorthLink vessel and route characteristics compared

	Pentland Ferries	NorthLink
	Gills Bay– *St Margaret's Hope*	*Scrabster–* *Stromness*
	Pentalina	*Hamnavoe*
Capital cost	£7 million	£30 million
Car capacity	78	95
Capital cost per car-space	£93,000	£316,000
Crew winter (summer)	10 (11)	36 (40)*
Route length (nautical miles)	15	28
Trip time (hours)	1	1.5
Peak return trips per week	24	19*
Route capacity (cars)	1,800	1,805
Service speed	16 knots	18 knots
Engine power (megawatts)	3.9	8.7
Fuel burn/crossing (litres)	708	2,757

* Since Serco takeover of NorthLink, crewing and off-peak trips have been reduced

The capacity to move cars across the Pentland Firth is identical in both cases. The difference in capital cost, however, is such that four *Pentalinas* could be purchased for the price of one *Hamnavoe*. *Pentalina*'s crewing is not far short of a quarter that of *Hamnavoe*, whose fuel burn per crossing is approaching four times that of *Pentalina*, hence the need for NorthLink's circa £10 million subsidy on this one route.

Andrew Banks echoed the words of Western Ferries' Andrew Wilson of four decades earlier: 'If I had NorthLink's subsidy, I could provide a *free* service and still become a rich man.'

This huge differential comes down to length of route and, crucially, vessel design, which poses the question: why is *Pentalina* so much more efficient than *Hamnavoe*?

The answer is that she is a catamaran and the brainchild of Scots Australian Stuart Ballantyne. His Queensland-based naval architectural and project management firm, Sea Transport Corporation, has developed medium-speed catamaran design and operation to a fine art with worldwide orders to his credit.

Pentalina is typical, featuring a high payload to power ratio. This gives an overwhelming competitive and environmental advantage over traditional monohull (i.e. single-hull ferries). In essence, *Pentalina* can carry almost the same volume of vehicles at the same speed as a traditional monohull, but with about half the installed power requirement. The low-resistance, twin-hull configuration creates a broad vehicle deck thereby maximising payload while minimising fuel burn per passenger or vehicle. The high tunnel height of the catamaran is specially designed to handle the wave conditions experienced on the Pentland Firth, and the four-engine, quadruple screw arrangement ensures a high level of redundancy in the event of an engine failure.

The Achilles heel of the monohull ferry is that it is inherently top heavy with passenger accommodation stacked above the vehicle deck. To counteract the inherent tendency to capsize, such vessels must carry water ballast to keep them upright, rather like some oversized Mr Blobby! This extra weight means that there is much more hull to push through the water even before the payload is added, hence the big difference in power requirement and fuel consumption.

A further disadvantage of many monohull ferries and cruise ships is that their high slab sides can make them difficult to manoeuvre in a crosswind and difficult to evacuate in an emergency, if listing. This latter point was highlighted in January 2012 by the wreck of the cruise ship *Costa Concordia* off Isola del Giglio off the west coast of Italy in which 32 lives were lost.

It is sometimes stated that catamarans are unsuitable for rough water operation. Well, for one thing, the Pentland Firth is no mill pond. More tellingly, Atlantic Marine Services' go-anywhere catamaran *Orca III* plies regularly to St Kilda in the open Atlantic and has even ventured to Rockall, Scotland's (and indeed the world's) most isolated islet, more than 160 miles (300km) west of St Kilda.

Some Further Startling Vessel Comparisons

If the huge difference in capital cost between *Pentalina* and *Hamnavoe* is thought to be an exceptional aberration, think again. Professor Baird made comparison with other recent monohull ferry orders by CMAL.

One such was the commissioning by CMAL in 2010 of the *Finlaggan*, a 21-crew, 85-car, 550-passenger ferry for Islay, at a cost of £25 million. For the same price, three 80-car, much less fuel-thirsty catamarans could have been built.

Then there was the case of the new 143-car, 700-passenger ferry *Loch Seaforth II* ordered in summer 2012 by CMAL for the Stornoway run at a cost of £43 million. For that price three 140-car rough-water catamarans could be built at a cost of around US$22 million (£14 million) each.

Again there is the strange case of the much vaunted CMAL 'hybrid' ferry. Funding for these vessels was announced in February 2011. The concept was unveiled to me, as a then Highland councillor, by CMAL as a breakthrough in 'green' ferry transport. Orders had been placed with Ferguson Shipbuilders of Port Glasgow for two of these 23-car, 150-passenger hybrid ferries, powered partly by batteries and partly by diesel engines. The idea was that, while the ferry is berthed overnight, the ship plugs into the shore mains electricity supply to charge the two lithium-ion battery banks which then supply power to the ship's electric propulsion motors.

The ensuing discussion between councillors and CMAL can be reconstructed along the following lines:

'Mmm; interesting. So the ship runs throughout the day on battery power?'

'Well no, not exactly. Only some 20 per cent of the power comes from the batteries. The rest comes from onboard diesel generators, but all in all there is a reduction in CO_2 and other emissions of about 20 per cent.'

'Does this percentage take into account the environmental cost of generating the mains electricity?'

'Well, ehm, no, but we are looking at the possibility of using energy from local wind, wave or solar systems to charge the batteries.'

'I see Western Ferries are building two new larger 40-car ferries at Cammel Laird in Liverpool for around £4 million apiece. What will each of these hybrid ferries cost?'

'£11 million each, but once the technology is proven we hope the cost will come down a bit.'

Professor Baird then carried out a detailed evaluation of the CMAL hybrid in comparison with an 'off-the-shelf' Sea Transport 35-metre catamaran. In short, the catamaran could carry 52 per cent more cars,

22 per cent faster, with 49 per cent less installed power per car space and at 38 per cent of the capital cost while emitting no more and probably less CO_2.

A subsequent article published in *Cruise and Ferry International* magazine stated: 'Compared with the Sea Transport Corporation catamaran, the "hybrid" ferry, therefore, offers no advantage in terms of installed power or power demand per car space, and hence achieves no environmental advantage over existing ferries as claimed by CMAL ... Given the opportunity to acquire similar small ferries at much reduced prices, the CMAL "hybrid" ferry also represents a considerable and unnecessary waste of scarce public resources.' All in all a pretty damning indictment.

Perhaps the best illustration of all this is Professor Baird's graphic, 'Ferry Procurement Comparisons'.

A Norwegian Insight
Sometimes those of us who seek a more cost-effective approach to Scottish ferry operations feel we are ploughing a lonely furrow and for little reward. It is heartening, therefore, to have our ideas affirmed by observers from outside the country. One such affirmation came to me out of the blue from a Norwegian ferry skipper, Captain Torgeir H. Røyset, whose observations on a trip to Bute and Cowal were revealing. These are paraphrased as follows:

'I was shocked by the level of inefficiency on this relatively new ferry (*Bute*), operation-wise. The ferry was moored with fore and aft spring lines, as well as bow and aft lines, like a cargo ship docking at a terminal. As you might know, in Norway we use the link-span itself for mooring the ferry, with a sort of 'shelf' on the ferry's end on which the link-span rests. The ferry's ramp connects with the link-span through a "pin" that fits a slot in the link-span.

'The cumbersome mooring operation on the *Bute* calls for a high crew number, probably three or four ABs, to make it run smoothly. On a Norwegian ferry the same size, there would normally be two ABs, or maybe one in the off-peak periods. Also, the ABs do the ticket sales either before departure or during the crossing. These two elements eliminate the need for linesmen and ticket salespeople onshore. In fact, very few of the Norwegian ferry routes have people working at the shore facilities, as it's not necessary.

Public Sector   **Private Sector**

£30 million 98 cars
NorthLink *Hamnavoe*   buys   **FOUR** x 80 cars catamarans
                                            = 320 cars total capacity

£24.5 million 85 cars
CMAL *Finlaggan*   buys   **THREE** x 80 cars catamarans
                                        = 240 cars total capacity

£43 million 143 cars
CMAL *Loch Seaforth*   buys   **THREE** x 140 cars rough-water
                                            catamarans = 420 cars cap

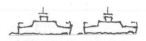

Two **£22 million** 23 cars each
CMAL 'Hybrid' ferries   buys   **FIVE** x 35 cars Sea Transport Co
                                             catamarans = 175 cars cap

Ferry Procurement Comparisons
Courtesy Professor Alfred Baird

'Also, why build ferries of this kind on a crossing of this length? They should be double-ended, with bow visors, but with a wider opening to speed up the unloading process of the ferry, unloading two lanes at the same time (if the link-span is wide enough, that is). You may know the Shetland Island Council's *Daggri* and *Dagalien* (see illustration) – two ferries of this kind, with a bit higher capacity, would be perfect on this crossing.

'After a wee bus ride, we came to the Rhubodach ferry slipway. I wasn't at all impressed with this layout, either. As a ferry navigator myself, it's easy to imagine the trouble in manoeuvring the ferry onto the slipway in stormy weather, with no quayside (aligning structure) to fall onto. I believe the Norwegian model would fit here also, by being able to moor the ferry via the link-span in all sorts of weather. Although it has to be said that this ferry was light years ahead of the aforementioned crossing, in terms of efficiency.

'The last trip was from Dunoon to Gourock on the *Saturn*. We were invited up on the bridge by the very friendly crew and got to see how highly manoeuvrable this ferry was. In terms of operation, though, I would say this was useless. Side-loading cars and mooring lines like on the *Bute* meant a crew of ten persons were kept busy. I believe this crossing is now out of business, with only Western Ferries left, doing it the Norwegian way.'

Captain Røyset was surprised at what he perceived as the high level of fares and the old-fashioned layout of the then new *Finlaggan*, of which he opined that the crew numbers and running costs were 'far too high'. He continued:

'To sum things up, Calmac's way of running things seems a bit strange to me. Either it's highly inefficient terminals and ferries (Wemyss Bay–Rothesay) or there's just a slipway and a basic ferry (Colintraive-Rhubodach). I don't know why they chose this separation of operation methods, but neither of them seem optimal to me. It certainly wouldn't have been accepted by the people of Western Norway. It should be mentioned that Calmac seem to have a very friendly and service-minded crew, both on the ships and on the terminals.

'When I returned to Norway, I Googled around and found your reports and comments on Calmac's inefficient ways, and I just wanted to give my support – you're absolutely right.'

Says it all, really. Apart from drawing attention to the general inefficiency of CalMac's ship design and operation, Captain Røyset highlights the inadequacies of both the heavy labour-intensive style of link-span used and the susceptibility of slipways to wind and swell issues. The standard Scandinavian ferry terminal, as employed by Shetland Islands Council and Western Ferries, features a link-span that locks onto the vessel, such that both can rise and fall with the swell. Not only is this arrangement inherently safer, but it is cheaper to install and requires minimal or no shore staff to operate.

One cannot but agree with Captain Røyset in wondering why this efficient technology was not adopted as standard in Scotland, as recommended by the Highland Transport Board nearly four decades ago. Is it yet too late to move in that direction?

An account of the development of Norwegian ferry policy is given in Chapter 4.

FUMING FERRIES

The reduction of harmful emissions from ships is one issue that has risen up the agenda, internationally and nationally. In fact the Scottish Government has well and truly nailed its colours to the mast of reducing the nation's carbon footprint under the terms of the Climate Change (Scotland) Act 2009. This act set ambitious targets to reduce Scotland's emissions of the basket of six Kyoto Protocol greenhouse gases by 42 per cent by 2020 and 80 per cent by 2050, compared to the 1990/1995 baseline. As well as domestic emissions, Scotland's share of emissions from aviation and shipping are included in the targets.

As recently as June 2012 the Conserve and Save: Energy Efficiency Action Plan reaffirmed the Scottish Government's approach to meeting Scotland's climate change targets and to securing the transition to a low-carbon economy in Scotland by significantly reducing carbon dioxide (CO_2) emissions. In doing so, it seeks to create employment, promote new technologies and secure wider economic benefits. Key actions relating to energy efficiency include reducing transport energy demand and transforming how the transport systems are used.

A few years back, the long black trail of engine exhaust belching from the Caledonian MacBrayne ferry *Clansman*'s funnel was what got me thinking about ferry emissions. *Clansman* was just passing Tobermory on passage from Lochboisdale to Oban with some 30 cars and a couple of trucks on her vehicle deck. For the next hour's steaming, the ferry would consume some 1,500 litres of fuel as she proceeded down the Sound of Mull, parallel to the 18-mile (29km) road between Tobermory and Craignure.

What would the vehicles on the ferry's deck consume if they were driven that distance, rather than being carried on the ship? It was a simple enough calculation. I reckoned that the average car consumed less than two litres to cover the distance. On that basis, 30 average cars would consume less than 60 litres collectively. Add, say, 50 litres for the two trucks and a coach to carry the foot passengers and 110 litres would more than suffice to convey *Clansman*'s entire payload down the Sound of Mull by road, and at twice the speed.

Clearly, with the load that day, *Clansman* consumed some *thirteen times* the fuel per kilometre as compared with moving the traffic by road. Even with a full load (a rare event), she would burn some seven times the road equivalent.

But that is not all. *Clansman* burns dirty heavy fuel oil (HFO) which emits more nasty nitrous, sulphur oxides and 'black carbon' than diesel and petrol and produces more CO_2 per litre than cleaner road fuels.

Black carbon, incidentally, has a major impact on some of the world's most fragile ecosystems including the Arctic and the Himalayan ice caps. It consists of extremely small particles (soot) from incomplete combustion of fossil fuels. Climate science now places black carbon in the top three warming agents along with CO_2 and methane. It is also a health hazard. Between 2,500 to 3,000 people in Scotland die each year from inhaling such pollutants compared with some 190 deaths annually from road accidents.

Bearing in mind the Scottish Government's laudable and much-vaunted ambitious targets for CO_2 reduction, *Clansman*'s performance in this regard seemed an affront these ambitions.

Researching Ferry Emissions

Some time later, in June 2010 in fact, I was asked to address the KIMO International Conference on the issue of ferry emissions. KIMO (Kommunenes Internasjonale Miljøorganisasjon) or Local Authorities International Environmental Organisation, is an influential body that engages with environmental threats using practical, diplomatic and research-based approaches.

The presentation set out key facts about CO_2 emissions and made comparisons between different ferry operations. First the key facts on the carbon footprint of a typical ferry:

- One megawatt of power consumes 220 litres per hour
- Burning one litre of marine diesel emits 2.64 kilograms of CO_2
- Burning one litre of heavy fuel oil emits 3.22 kilograms of CO_2

The presentation then considered two locations where private and state-owned vehicle ferry operators were in competition at that time. The first area considered was the upper Firth of Clyde between Cowal and Inverclyde where at the time Western Ferries and CalMac ran competing services. The following table summarises the relative vessel characteristics and performance:

Vessel and route performance comparison between Cowal and Inverclyde

	Western Ferries	CalMac
	Hunter's Quay–McInroy's Point	Dunoon-Gourock
VESSELS		
Car capacity	45	40
Crew	4	10
Engine power	0.89 MW	1.5 MW
Passage distance	2.5 miles	4.25 miles
PERFORMANCE		
Passengers/yr	1,307,000	615,200
Cars/yr	577,800	77,800
CVs/yr	33,700	6,000
Fuel/yr	1,180 tonnes	1,212 tonnes
CO_2 per vehicle	6.0kg	44.8kg
Profit/Loss	£1.5 million Profit	£2.4 million Loss

2010 official figures

It will be observed that the Western Ferries vessels, with greater carrying capacity, had less than half the crew and about half the power. However they carried over eight times the vehicular traffic and with *one seventh* of the CO_2 emissions per vehicle, and at a profit to boot, compared with the CalMac loss-making operation. The CalMac vehicle ferry has since been withdrawn. In a nutshell, the overwhelming advantage of the Western Ferries operation has been economical vessel design and operation and, crucially, a shorter and more frequent crossing.

The second location considered was the Pentland Firth covered in *Pentland Hero*. A comparison between Pentland Ferries and North-Link showed that the CO_2 emissions per car carried by unsubsidised operator Pentland Ferries' *Pentalina* are *one quarter* those of heavily subsidised *Hamnavoe* on the parallel NorthLink service. Again better vessel design, more economical operation and a shorter crossing are key explanations for the greatly superior performance.

Another issue covered at the KIMO conference was the decision of the IMO to adopt stricter controls on air pollution emissions by ships, with a focus on the high sulphur content of heavy fuel oil. Since that time the European Parliament's Environmental Committee has voted in favour of even stricter standards to be implemented by 2015. *Pentalina* already meets these standards. The NorthLink and large CalMac vessels do not.

These findings were conveyed to officials of Transport Scotland (the Scottish Government's transport agency) as part of the Scottish Ferries Review that was proceeding at that time. It was a surprise, therefore, that NorthLink, apparently with Scottish Government blessing, announced increased freight frequency on the Aberdeen–Kirkwall route claiming that, 'the shift of lorries from road to water on their Aberdeen–Kirkwall freight service helps the Scottish Government in achieving its carbon reduction targets'. This claim proved to be wholly unfounded.

The St Margaret's Hope Study

The St Margaret's Hope Pier trustees certainly had their doubts. They saw this heavily subsidised diversion of freight traffic from Pentland Ferries and their port as a threat. To test their opinion, the trustees commissioned Professor Alf Baird and myself to investigate and compare the performance of ferry services between the Scottish mainland

and Orkney, together with surface transport connections, in terms of CO_2 emissions. The studies were undertaken to inform the 'Carbon Account for Transport' which helps government to take decisions and develop actions to meet the targets of the Climate Change (Scotland) Act 2009.

The approach was in essence an extended and more detailed version of the KIMO presentation. It focussed on ferries serving three routes: Aberdeen–Kirkwall, Scrabster–Stromness and Gills Bay–St Margaret's Hope.

In the first instance we calculated ferry CO_2 emissions and fuel consumption per trailer, per car and per passenger. We then calculated the connecting land transport CO_2 emissions for each route and mode (trailer, car, bus and train), between a common southern destination (Edinburgh) and each of the Scottish mainland ports. Finally we summed overland and ferry transport legs, to give the total level of CO_2 emissions per trip. The ratio of CO_2 emissions on the passenger/vehicle ferries attributable to freight, cars and passengers were allocated broadly in proportion to the ship space and revenues derived in each case.

The results were startling. In terms of freight traffic the studies demonstrated clearly that, rather than reducing emissions on the transport of freight to and from Orkney, the Aberdeen route actually generates significantly more CO_2 per trailer than the longer landward road journey, coupled with the frequent short sea crossing of the Pentland Firth operated by Pentland Ferries, as follows:

Road plus Gills Bay–St Margaret's Hope on *Pentalina*   869kg CO_2
Road plus Aberdeen–Kirkwall on cargo ship *Helliar*   1,483kg CO_2
Road plus Aberdeen–Kirkwall on passenger ferry *Hjaltland*   5,646kg CO_2

The Scottish Government's promotion of the increased frequency of NorthLink's Aberdeen–Kirkwall freight service was clearly at odds with its own ambitious plans to reduce CO_2 emissions by increasing them instead.

The results for the overall journey between Edinburgh and Orkney by cars with different numbers of accompanying passengers and for passengers using bus or train and ferry were even more telling. The following comparative table for CO_2 emissions for car with driver covering the overall journey between Edinburgh and Orkney by road and ferry illustrates the outcome. The difference in CO_2 emissions northbound and southbound on the Aberdeen route is because the northbound vessel utilises all four fuel-thirsty engines to achieve 24 knots. Southbound, two engines only suffice for the 16-knot overnight passage.

Overall CO_2 comparison: Edinburgh–Orkney by accompanied car and ferry

	Ferry		Road	Total
	CO_2/trip kg	CO_2/car &Pass'g'r kg	CO_2/car &Pass'g'r kg	CO_2 kg
Aberdeen–Kirkwall northbound	65,133	803	21	824
Aberdeen–Kirkwall southbound	54,819	676	21	697
Scrabster–Stromness	8,877	184	43	227
Gills Bay– St Margaret's Hope	1,892	48	44	92

It will be seen that the overall journey via the NorthLink Aberdeen route northbound emits up to *nine times* the CO_2 per car plus passenger compared with Pentland Ferries Gills Bay route, and the Scrabster route emits some *two and a half times* the CO_2. A similar picture emerged for ferry plus other combinations of bus or train. It was particularly remarkable that for the Aberdeen route, in all cases, travel by air emitted less CO_2 per passenger.

These findings were sent by the St Margaret's Hope Pier trustees to the Scottish Government in the spring of 2011. In May 2012 the findings were presented by Professor Alf Baird and myself at the Eighth Scottish Transport Applications and Research Conference (STAR 2012) held at the Lighthouse in Glasgow and sponsored by Transport Scotland. We were honoured with the best paper prize.

Next came the Orkney Science Festival. Although it was nine in the evening, there was a good turnout. Alf and I did a double act, covering the issue of CO_2 emissions more or less as set out above.

That afternoon we had checked the total demand in Orkney for electricity. It was 15.76 megawatts. Renewable energy generated that windy day was 20.92 megawatts. There were gasps in the audience when I pointed out that northbound the *Hjaltland* and *Hrossay* serving the Aberdeen–Orkney route had a power output of 21.6 megawatts. This is a power requirement greater than the entire Orkney demand for electricity and which also neutralises Orkney's entire renewable energy generation. There were further gasps when it was pointed out that the Aberdeen route subsidy appeared to be the world's highest, equivalent to some £350 per return passenger carried, yet the route accounted for only 8 per cent of passengers and cars travelling between mainland Scotland and Orkney.

We were asked what response the St Margaret's Hope Pier trustees had had on this important issue from Transport Scotland, the answer was: 'None!'

The lessons that come through very clearly from this research into ship emissions are very clear. To reduce emissions it is necessary to concentrate traffic on the shortest feasible ferry crossing and employ efficient vessels with good payload characteristics and low fuel consumption.

CREWING EXCESSES

With few exceptions it has to be said that the public face of the state-funded operators in terms of their 'front of house' personnel and crews is one of friendly courtesy. The huge disparity in crewing levels, however, between operators like Western Ferries and Pentland Ferries on the one hand and CalMac and NorthLink on the other has already been alluded to.

No operator is of course allowed to put a vessel to sea with less than a safe manning level. The penalties for doing so are severe. Safe manning levels for any vessel are determined by the MCA in accordance with IMO rules. It may be asked why it is that *Pentalina* can run with a crew of 10 while NorthLink's *Hamanavoe* has a minimum crew of 28 and, at least in state-owned days, commonly a crew of up to 40. The answer lies in vessel design, the number of passengers the ship is designed to carry, and ease of evacuation in an emergency.

If a ship such as *Hamnavoe* is designed to accommodate 600

passengers she will require a very much larger crew than one, such as *Pentalina*, designed for 250. And yet it will be noted that *Pentalina* by virtue of the shorter, more frequent crossing she plies is able to cater for a similar traffic level. As crewing is one the main costs in running a ship, it is obvious that if one vessel carries one third the crew complement of another, there will be a massive difference in operating costs.

A further consideration is whether the crew live on board or ashore. If the crew is shore-based, it is a relatively straightforward matter to operate a shift system, as is the case with Shetland Islands Council ferries, thereby enabling vessels to operate for, say, 18 hours per day. This would not be possible with a live-aboard crew, as it would breach hours of work regulations, unless two crews were carried. Furthermore, accommodating live-aboard crews takes up valuable payload space on the vessel. The great advantage of shore-based crewing, where the ferry is based at the island it serves, is that it facilitates the recruitment of local labour and is, therefore, both family friendly and beneficial to the local economy.

Number of crew is one thing. Wage levels are another. The seagoing employees of the David MacBrayne Group of companies enjoy unusually favourable terms and conditions – high wages and 'gold-plated' for officers pensions who, it seems, work a fortnight on and a fortnight off with 10 weeks holiday in addition, i.e. a 21-week year! And all at public expense too. These terms are far better than those enjoyed by the vast majority of working people.

Bob the Gob

It is of course a trade union's job to protect the pay and conditions of its members. This is clearly the stated aim of the RMT, the National Union of Rail, Maritime and Transport Workers, whose even more generously paid general secretary Bob Crow threatened strike action if the forthcoming tender for Clyde and Hebrides (i.e. CalMac) routes were to be 'unbundled'.

Most people nowadays would celebrate the role of the trade union movement in the late nineteenth and much of the twentieth centuries in winning decent conditions and fair pay for a fair day's work. When a trade union seeks to preserve excessive privilege at the expense of the less fortunate, its validity weakens.

In his article 'Why Unions Need to Join the Real World' (*Herald*, 16

P&O Ferries' 40-knot catamaran *Express* at speed passing Corsewall Point. Scotland's fastest vehicle ferry. (Photo: Author)

Western Ferries' *Sound of Shuna* at McInroy's Point's Norwegian style 'lock-on' link span. Scotland's busiest car ferry, all without any subsidy. (Photo: Author)

Highland Council's *MV Corran*, Scotland's second busiest internal route. Simple, efficient and covers costs from the fare box. Note quarter loading ramps. (Photo: courtesy Highland Council)

CalMac's *Clansman* departing from Castlebay, Barra. Note the heavy link-span and emission of black carbon. At around £300 per round-trip passenger subsidy, this is one of the world's most heavily subsidised ferry routes. (Photo: Author)

CalMac's *Loch Alainn* at Eriskay slipway. The powers that be were astonished by the huge jump in traffic as compared with the longer service this route replaced. (Photo: Author)

Daggri and the simple 'lock-on' Norwegian style link-span terminal. Shetland Islands Council efficiency on Yellsound. (Photo: courtesy Shetland Islands Council)

Orkney Ferries' North Isles ferry *Varagen* at Kirkwall. (Photo: Author)

NorthLink's £30 million chronically uneconomic and polluting *Hamnavoe* at the £20 million Scrabster terminal. (Photo: Author)

Pentland Ferries' £7 million profitable and environmentally friendly *Pentalina* berthing at the £2 million Gills Bay terminal. (Photo: Author)

MacCallum Orme's *Dunara Castle* in the Sound of Iona. Hebridean stalwart for seven decades, and no mistaking that she was a coal-burner. (Photo: Author's Collection)

St Clair, the last steam ship built for the North of Scotland Orkney and Shetland SN Co. leaving Aberdeen for Lerwick. An oil burner. (Photo: Author)

Paddle Steamer *Waverley* at Iona. Last of the breed and still steaming. (Photo: Author)

Motor Ship Development

Derrick-loading motor vessel *Locheil* at West Loch Tarbert. (Photo: Author)

Firth of Clyde car ferry *Arran* – a step forward, but not a major advance. Vehicles were side-loaded by means of the hoist located just aft of the funnel. (Photo: Author's Collection)

'Open wide': Western Ferries' revolutionary drive-through *Sound of Jura*. (Photo: courtesy John Newth)

Glenachulish; Scotland's last turntable ferry operating between Glenelg and Kylerhea (Skye). (Photo: Undiscovered Scotland)

Go-anywhere 16-metre catamaran, *Orca III,* operated by Atlantic Marine Services. She runs regularly to St Kilda. (Photo: courtesy of operator Angus Campbell of Atlantic Marine Services and Frank Kowalski of builders Safehaven Marine)

Moss–Horten shuttle: a typical Norwegian *pendelferje*. (Photo: Author)

Aussie chic, SeaLink Kangaroo Island 16-knot, 378-passenger, 55-car catamaran ferry *Sealion 2000*. (Photo: courtesy SeaLink)

Foveaux Express arriving at Oban, the tiny capital of New Zealand's Stewart Island. (Photo: Author)

The first of ten new 49-metre Sea Transport Corporation 50-car ferries for the Philippines at about US$8.5m (£5.5m) per vessel. Speed on trials was 18.1 knots. Variants of these could easily be built in and for Scotland. (Photo: courtesy of Stuart Ballantine)

The Author (centre) and Professor Alf Baird (right) being presented with best paper prize at the May 2012 STAR Conference. The topic was ferry CO_2 emissions. (Photo: Stephen Hosey)

September 2012), Iain Macwhirter quoted Bob Crow's speech at the TUC conference: 'If you spit on your own, you can't do anything, but if you all spit together you can drown the bastards.' Macwhirter went on to say: 'When Bob the Gob opens his mouth, he doesn't realise that many members of the public think he is spitting at them.'

What is worrying about the undue influence of the RMT is first their threat of strike action and a campaign of political and public pressure, alongside the David MacBrayne Group's own efforts to pressurise the Scottish Government to abandon the idea set out in the ferries consultation document of separately tendering a number of routes. The second concern is that in September 2012 Scottish ministers so quickly acquiesced to the RMT's demand. The Scottish Government also announced that the competition to run the west coast ferries, currently operated by CalMac, was to be postponed for three years.

Not unnaturally Bob Crow was jubilant, saying: 'The three-year delay on the CalMac tendering is a massive victory for the RMT campaign against privatisation and in defence of jobs and working conditions. There is no question that our campaign of political and public pressure, alongside a massive mandate for strike action from our members, has helped force the pace on this momentous decision.'

This is all well and good for the privileged RMT members, but Scottish ferry services are not a job-creation scheme. If the result of appeasement of the RMT is over-manned vessels on services that do not properly meet the best needs of the communities they serve, then public funding is fated to rise. This will divert funds from other much-needed public services. This is not in the public interest.

The next target of the RMT was Serco NorthLink who were under fire from the union for seeking to shed 36 posts from their Scrabster–Stromness and Aberdeen–Orkney and Shetland routes. One can hardly blame Serco when it is realised that for the whole of February 2012, for example, the number of passengers per crossing on the Scrabster–Stromness route averaged fewer than 30 souls (on a ship crewed for 600 passengers). What is the point of employing a multitude of highly paid chefs, stewards and ratings, when customers are fewer in number than the crew? It does, therefore, seem that Serco's plan to adopt the kind of flexible crewing that is standard practice with most ferry operators is the only sensible way forward. Of course the RMT did not view it that way. Their press release announced:

'Shipping union RMT today slammed deliberately provocative comments from the Managing Director of Serco NorthLink that he will attempt to run a seriously understaffed scab service in the event of a vote for strike action in a ballot over staffing cuts.'

Next in line was Orkney Ferries, where a claim was submitted to the company for a substantial increase in rates of pay and improvements to conditions of service. RMT representatives were advised by Orkney Ferries' management that a pay freeze for 2012 and a 1 per cent increase in 2013 was the best they could offer, although they would consider a self-financed offer, such that any increase in basic pay must be funded by savings in other costs of employment. This was rejected, and RMT declared a dispute and began balloting for strike action.

The clichéd and exaggerated language of the RMT was again quaintly reminiscent of a satirical farce: 'RMT will not stand back while our members' standards of living are driven to poverty levels with this *de facto* freezing of pay rates well off into the future.'

Bearing in mind the relatively generous levels of pay enjoyed by Orkney Ferries' employees, the concept of 'poverty-level' pay hardly rings true when there are so many other hard-working people in much less privileged positions. So a more realistic phrasing might be 'tightening the belt a little' – just like the rest of us.

It is of course a trade union's role to seek good working conditions, but to seek to force government to change the direction of policy against the wider public interest is blackmail.

SHORT CROSSING THEORY

The advantages of shortest feasible passage for a ferry crossing and road equivalence has been mentioned several times. In fact the concept is a key means of reducing capital costs, fuel consumption and emissions and crewing.

In this connection it is perhaps worth relating that in January 2008 I gave a presentation to the Chartered Institute of Logistics and Transport entitled 'Cost-effective Ferries' describing the concept of road equivalence and 'ferry impedance'. This presentation was a development of an earlier exposition given at the Orkney Science Festival in 2007 which drew on a long series of research reports inspired originally by seminal Norwegian work dating back to the early 1960s.

To explain road equivalence in terms of ferries: roads are the universal transport mode connecting virtually everywhere with everywhere except where water intervenes. Then, ferries act as a floating bridge. However traffic on a ferry crossing is always less than if there had been an actual road (or fixed link) across that stretch of water. This constraining effect of a ferry crossing is defined as 'impedance'. The degree of impedance can vary greatly depending on:

- Passage time (a function of distance or speed)
- Frequency
- Hours of operation
- Price (by no means the most important)

The pursuit of road equivalence seeks to make ferry crossings as 'road-like' as possible, thereby reducing the impedance effect. Thus shortening routes automatically has the positive consequence of simultaneously reducing passage time, increasing frequency and constraining price. It has the multiple effect of radically reducing impedance and greatly increasing traffic flows on the route, thereby facilitating social and economic benefit to the community served. A further benefit is reduced operating cost and increased revenue, which may permit extending hours of operation and further social and economic benefit at no extra cost to the public purse.

When the long, infrequent passages connecting Harris with North Uist and South Uist with Barra were replaced with smaller more frequent ferries across the shorter 'Sounds', CalMac and the then Scottish Office/Executive were astonished by the huge jump in traffic as compared with the longer services they replaced. They should not have been surprised. Impedance had been reduced and road equivalence more closely achieved.

A ferry crossing acts as a bridge between island and mainland or between island and island. Relatively little traffic originates at, or is destined for, the port at either end of the passage. Most traffic is involved in longer transits, in which case it makes sense for the choice of the terminal ports to be determined by operational cost effectiveness rather than by historical accident or local political pressure.

It may be argued that islands and peninsular communities are where they are and you can't alter geography. In fact, as highlighted by the

Highland Transport Board and others, there are many opportunities to shorten sea passages in ways that would bring much benefit to communities, while reducing public expenditure. How this can be done in practice is described in Chapter 5.

FAIR FARES

About twenty-five years ago on the two-and-a-quarter-hour ferry crossing between Cedar Island and Okracoke, North Carolina, I fell into conversation with a local passenger who complained to me about the, then, $10 driver and vehicle charge (now $15). When I explained that for a similar journey in Scotland the charge would be at least ten times as much, the retort was, 'Gee! How do folks live there?'

The lesson was that no matter how cheap the ferry fare is, people will still complain.

The fares hitherto charged on Scottish state-subsidised ferries have been inconsistent. As previously mentioned, they are but one of the factors facilitating or inhibiting movement, other factors being passage time, frequency, operating hours and convenience of timings. Thus a shorter, more frequent crossing operating into the late evening may generate more traffic than reducing fares. The rationale for a fares policy, when combined with the other above-mentioned factors should be community sustainability through promotion of economic development (including tourism where appropriate) and social well-being while minimising environmental damage and cost to the public purse. This means striking a balance.

Fares have the greatest negative impact on long routes where frequencies also tend to be low. On shorter routes, the current general level of fares presents much less of a barrier to patronage, as demonstrated by the figures below which represent the number of passengers travelling (passengers' propensity to travel) per head of island population. Examples in round numbers are:

Cumbrae (very frequent)	700
Mull (several crossings per day)	300
Lewis (two longish round trips per day)	10
Shetland (long nightly route via Aberdeen)	5

Thus there would seem to be a *prima facie* case for concentrating a low fares policy on the relatively few long routes rather than blanket coverage throughout Scotland.

So in 2008 the Scottish Government introduced RET (road equivalent tariff) on ferry services to and from the Western Isles, Coll and Tiree, greatly reducing fares. This action was taken as pilot scheme, in view of the economic difficulties and high level of out-migration then being experienced in the Outer Hebrides. The scheme was based on a formula whereby cars were charged a flat fee of £5 plus 60p per mile of passage. Passengers were charged £2 plus 10p per mile. On long routes the mileage charge was further reduced where RET would have resulted in fares at a level greater than the pre-existing tariff.

There were howls from Orkney and Shetland politicians protesting that their comparatively prosperous communities were being discriminated against. I was asked to appear on *Newsnight Scotland* to give a view. Having been the architect of RET as far back as 1974 (see Chapter 2), I waved my original report in front of the camera to explain that in fact the fares between Aberdeen and the Northern Isles for passengers, cars and commercial vehicles were already less than RET level. I wondered if the Northern Isles politicians were seeking a fares increase!

When the Western Isles trial had run its course, it was found that, while passenger and car traffic had increased, commercial vehicle traffic had remained more or less static and there were accusations that hauliers had not passed on savings to customers. As a result, RET was retained for passengers and cars, but not for hauliers. There was further discontent at this.

The Scottish Government then announced that RET would be extended to other island communities. When it was extended to Islay, there were again protests from local politicians that the fares were still not cheap enough!

There is undoubtedly a sense in many island communities that their local economy is strangled by ferry charges, but bearing in mind that ferry subsidies are already at unsustainable levels, it is difficult to justify blanket cheap fares unless much greater operational efficiency can be achieved. There are ways of doing that, as will be demonstrated, but the big question is whether or not there is the will to bring about the radical change in policy required to achieve this end.

FERRY MAFIA

A reasonable person might think that the powers that be would be somewhat taken aback, eager to know more, anxious to find a new way forward that would mitigate the undoubted flaws in current practice. But no. It seems, with some honourable exceptions, that officialdom's first impulse is to ignore the source of demonstrable, if embarrassing, facts in the hope that they will go away.

If the purveyor of the troublesome facts does not go away, the next instinct is to try to discredit the messenger. In my experience, and I have witnessed many examples, this is rarely done to the critic's face. It is done, rather, through what can only be described as an off-the-record, 'nudge-nudge' campaign of innuendo, ridicule and even complaint to the critic's superiors or client base. This has certainly been the experience of many whistle-blowers who have taken the trouble to demonstrate that there are serious problems with the way Scottish ferries are organised and operated.

Suppression of Data

Nor is this phenomenon linked with any one shade of political administration. They are all guilty. For decades, opposition politicians have sought route-by-route subsidy figures for CalMac's services, while CalMac, with ministerial support (whether Conservative, Labour, Liberal Democrat or SNP), has refused to reveal these. What has been perpetrated for the last four decades is a system of subsidisation without public accountability.

This was exemplified by recent exchanges in the Scottish Parliament. On 12 September 2012 Jim Hume MSP asked the Scottish Government what the operating deficit was on each Caledonian MacBrayne/CalMac Ferries Ltd route in 2007, 2008, 2009, 2010 and 2011.

The answer by Keith Brown MSP, Minister for Transport and Veterans, was short: 'Data on Scottish Government support for ferry services are not broken down by route.'

It seems incredible to the point of utter incompetence that a business the size of Caledonian MacBrayne Ferries does not know how its revenues and costs are broken down. Or is it that they do know, but have something to hide? Perhaps the revelation that *all* the company's routes made losses was just too embarrassing.

One unusual occasion on which route-by-route losses were published was the Caledonian MacBrayne Annual Report of 2005–2006. The data for 2007 and the three previous years were again made available to MSPs in 2008 in the parliament by Transport Minister Stewart Stevenson in response to a question by Jim Tolson MSP with the qualification that: 'Since 2007–08 [the information] is not recorded on an individual route basis.'

The brief period of openness was over, and just when such data would have been helpful in informing the Scottish Government's consultation on ferries.

As an aid to understanding the issue, Appendix 3 sets out the last published route deficit figures (those for 2007). Then taking the passenger carryings by route (as indicated in Appendix 1) the calculated subsidy per round trip passenger is listed alongside. By extrapolating from the overall increase in subsidy since that time, an updated notional subsidy per round trip passenger per route has, in addition, been estimated for 2011.

One of the fundamental difficulties with the system of funding Scottish ferries is the near-monopolistic hold the David MacBrayne Group (DMG) and CMAL have over policy and the way in which this inhibits innovation and results in poor value for money. There is much in the modus operandi of the DMG in particular and its relationship with government officials that has occasioned concern but that has never been addressed in a frank and open way in any formal review. Adam Smith had a good deal to say about the dangers of monopoly. Among them was the truism: 'Monopoly is a great enemy to good management.' These words are as true today as in the time of the pioneer economist.

It is a characteristic of monopolies that they seek to preserve and expand their function. From statements made and actions taken by the component companies of the DMG, that group is no exception. With self-preservation and expansion as the motivation, maximising public funding becomes the easiest way of achieving growth with little heed being paid to controlling labour and other costs, so long as the growing disparity between costs and outcomes does not become too obvious. To conceal this disparity, the group has adopted a policy of suppression of useful data. In contrast to the secrecy of the DMG, the local authorities are quite open about releasing such data to public scrutiny.

There is surely a strong argument that, as taxpayers are paying well in excess of £100 million per annum to publicly funded operators; they are entitled to know exactly what they are getting for their money. Whatever the advantage to the employees of David MacBrayne Group, it is clearly not in the public interest for route-by-route statistics to be withheld. These services are *not* commercial. In view of this block on scrutiny, and to enable public understanding of the value for money (or lack of it) of ferry services, it should surely be a condition of government funding that all ferry operators so funded publish route-by-route data on carryings, revenues and subsidies.

There was a glimmer of hope that perhaps the powers that be might be open to more enlightened ideas following the publication of the National Transport Strategy in 2006, when it was announced that there was to be a serious look at Scottish ferries policy.

One of the first signs of activity was an enquiry by Scottish Parliament's Transport, Infrastructure and Climate Change Committee. Having myself been elected to the Highland Council in May 2007, I was able as Vice-Chair of Transport, Environmental and Community Services to give evidence both in that capacity and privately in March 2008 in the form of a detailed paper entitled 'A Better Way to Run Ferries', which outlined many of the ideas described in this book.

In the event, little emerged from that committee's deliberations, but the Scottish Government did embark upon what was described as a 'route and branch' review of, and consultation on, Scottish ferry services.

As the Ferries Review Consultation progressed, concerns emerged about the secrecy and lobbying clout of the David MacBrayne Group in skewing the consultation process in favour of preserving as much of the status quo as possible.

In February 2009 a Scottish Government official stated: 'In setting in place the management and consultative arrangements for the review we [officials of the Scottish Government] have been careful to ensure that those who might benefit commercially from future tendering arrangements e.g. CalMac Ferries Ltd and NorthLink Ferries, are not part of the Steering Group managing the study nor leading on policy development.'

Rather than an 'arm's length' relationship, however, it seems in fact that representatives of these operators have been very heavily involved, at public expense, in local consultation meetings and in seeking to influence stakeholders in favour of their schemes. Many stakeholders have little knowledge of ferry economics. The absence of route-by-route traffic and cost statistics clearly aids such lobbying bias by removing, from other than the most informed stakeholders, the tools for critical analysis.

Notwithstanding this block on data, it is a relatively straightforward matter for an analyst familiar with ferry operations to estimate costs and revenue on a route-by-route basis. The key data can be uncovered by a bit of detective work, viz:

- Vessel crewing as stated on each vessel's passenger certificate
- As wages and conditions are generally known, it is therefore possible to calculate crewing costs
- Vessel power output as listed in Lloyd's Register of Shipping from which it is possible to calculate fuel burn
- As fuel price is known, it is then possible to calculate fuel costs
- Capital costs of vessels, terminals and roads have generally been published from which an annualised capital value can be set
- Timetables are published from which vessel operating hours can be estimated
- Fares and charges are published, as are annual traffic figures from which revenue can be estimated, allowing for child and other discounts
- Industry norms can be applied to estimate other costs such as insurance, overhaul, etc.

It would just be so much easier and more accurate for such data to be published. Unless such calculations are made and compared, route by route, for current services and for alternative operating scenarios, it is not possible to get a realistic feel for where inefficiencies may lie and improvement may be made. It is difficult to understand why in the course of the lengthy and hugely expensive ferries review such an exercise was not carried out by costing and comparing existing operations with alternative scenarios.

This problem of DMG secrecy, and the apparent collusion with government officials in maintaining it, is a deep-seated one that goes back a long way to the days of STG ownership of CalMac. As far back as the 1970s, the frustrating experience of Western Ferries has already been described.

Arrogance

Around that time too, when I was a young transport research officer with the Highlands and Islands Development Board, I was scheduled to meet a Scottish Office official and a senior manager of what I shall loosely call the CalMac family. The meeting was about allegations (true, as it transpired) that MacBrayne Haulage, an STG subsidiary, was getting preferential rates on CalMac ferries, so giving an unfair advantage over other haulage firms. The official and I were picked up in central Glasgow by the said manager in his car to be taken to his club to meet over lunch.

As we sped off, and after initial pleasantries, I was astonished to hear the manager utter the words:

'I hope none of you are Catholics.'

The Scottish Office official was quick to answer:

'Oh no, certainly not.'

Having been brought up in the north-east of Scotland where sectarian bigotry is absent and indeed abhorred, I remained silent on the grounds that one's religious affiliations, if any, are nobody's business but one's own. I didn't have the presence of mind to ask: 'Why what would happen?'

We arrived at the manager's 'club' which was located in Ibrox – the Rangers Football Club. What came across during that meeting was a sense of untouchable self-importance which was not dispelled by subsequent dealings with CalMac.

The DMG/CalMac management are expert at spreading a positive image through Rotary clubs, masonic lodges, community and business groups, wining and dining councillors, officials and other influencers and anyone they think they can bring on side. Most of all they have clearly worked hard to build very close, many would say cosy, relationships with Scottish Government officials. The cost of such efforts is unknown.

There was the case of the MV *Hebrides* delivered in 2000 which was too big for the existing Uig pier, necessitating a costly extension on the part of Highland Council.

Then, as already described, there was the Northern Isles tender won by NorthLink, a CalMac joint venture, on the basis that the initial annual subsidy of £10.8 million would shrink to £7.8 million by the fifth year, only to be bailed out by no less than £35.7 million before the bundle of routes could be re-tendered. One would expect such demonstrable financial incompetence to rule out that operator from any future tender, but who won the job? Yes, NorthLink, restructured as a wholly owned CalMac subsidiary.

In 2010 the debacle over the new Islay ferry *Finlaggan* being unable to berth at the terminals she was supposed to serve, without many millions of pounds of additional expenditure, exposed the utter ineptitude of all concerned. In addressing criticism of this fiasco, the culture of breathtaking arrogance was demonstrated when CalMac's then Managing Director Phil Preston was on record as saying: 'The only experts worth listening to are our own' (i.e. CalMac's).

A particularly embarrassing event, also in 2010, was the resignation of the company's head of human resources, 'to pursue new career challenges', after *Scotland on Sunday* had revealed he had been forced to repay nearly £13,000 in expenses. Accountants had reported that the individual had charged more than £5,000 in takeaway meals and £1,200 on off-licence bills to CalMac, a goodly proportion being 'within close proximity' of the individual's large house in Bearsden. He had used his corporate MasterCard to pay for his son's application to university clearing system UCAS. Other claims queried included £1,750 for five-star hotels, a bill of more than £900 made up to his wife, and £137 for a crystal figurine. The accountants pointed out that some claims were written up as being payable for meals taken on weekdays, although receipts had weekend or evening dates. A company spokesman was reported to have said:

'We are entirely satisfied that there was no intention to defraud.' But he also added that the individual had accepted that some of his claims were 'inappropriate'.

To be fair, many well-run companies suffer 'irregularities' at the hands of employees, but when the person concerned is the head of human resources, it does call into question that individual's commitment to hard negotiation in terms of containing labour costs.

Lobbying

The lobbying clout of the David MacBrayne Group in influencing the consultation process in favour of preserving as much of the status quo as possible has been noted. Listening to lobbying is one thing, but succumbing to it is a weakness; seeking direction from self-interested lobbyists is potentially dangerous. It's somewhat akin to asking Al Capone how to crack the crime wave.

In making decisions, politicians take careful note of lobbying by local and other interests. It is, however, undoubtedly true that many, perhaps most, communities fear change and seek to preserve the familiar if inefficient practices of the past. This was true in Shetland when the plans were announced in 1960 to replace the thrice-weekly *Earl of Zetland* with the now indispensable frequent overland system. How many Shetlanders today would welcome a return to the old regime? Orcadians were against the introduction of RO-RO on the Pentland Firth but quickly came to recognise its benefits once introduced. This is essentially the situation with Islay and Jura and with Coll and Tiree and elsewhere where the opportunity arises to replace infrequent long routes with better roads and frequent short connecting ferry shuttles, yet such schemes are viewed by sections of the local communities as in some way the end of civilisation!

Dissenting voices will undoubtedly be raised in fierce opposition to some of the recommendations for change contained in Chapter 5. It is natural for communities to resist change and lobby hard to preserve what is no longer defensible. This is a fact of political life but at times the wider public interest is served by taking a more detached view and overriding loud self-interested lobbying where it is not justified. This takes leadership, political skill and informed and reasoned argument.

Notable examples include the small but vociferous Dunoon lobby which, despite having Scotland's busiest and most road equivalent service available to them without public subsidy, seek to reinstate a vehicle ferry on the nearly parallel but longer town-centre-to-town-centre Gourock route despite the fact that it is uneconomic, environmentally damaging, contrary to EU state aids rules and would require enhanced subsidy. The current town centre passenger service gives the desired, if lightly used, rail connection, but why land vehicles in the town centre? Transport policy is normally geared to *removing* all but the most necessary vehicles from town centres. Fears of Western Ferries raising fares once subsidised competition was removed have not materialised. In fact as befits the shorter crossing, Western Ferries passenger fares are cheaper than those on the longer subsidised passenger service.

Another such is the Stromness lobby which seeks to maintain the extremely heavily subsidised but underutilised Scrabster link when the more efficient unsubsidised service exists on the shorter, cheaper, more frequent crossing between St Margaret's Hope and Gills Bay.

One of the most curious cases is that of Port Ellen, where there was a strong lobby to retain that port, when Port Askaig offered a shorter crossing and better access for Jura. The main justification was that some other islands had more than one port with mainland links. That is true, but none has two ports linked with the SAME mainland terminal.

Then there are some operating companies themselves, particularly in the public sector, who may find it most comfortable to preserve the status quo and devote a good deal of effort and taxpayers' money to resisting uncomfortable change. Bill Bonner of *Money Weekly* sums it up neatly: 'Lobbying is not productive behavior. It does not lead to higher output. It does not fund innovation or new inventions. It does not pay new workers nor stimulate additional sales.'

Policy makers should take note.

HIGH HOPES DASHED

As the Scottish Government's Ferries Review commenced, the newly elected SNP Highland Council administration was seeking to unlock the potential of the moribund former Nigg oil platform construction yard on the shores of the Cromarty Firth for use 'mainly as a marine heavy engineering complex'. While this was being considered, Pentland Ferries was taking delivery of the new catamaran *Pentalina* whose construction and operating costs were so much less than an equivalent traditional CalMac ferry. It was Professor Alf Baird who 'joined the dots' and suggested the assembly of *Pentalina*-type catamarans at Nigg.

So it was, in September 2008, that Alf and I met local Councillor Maxine Smith at a roadside café at Tomich on the A9 to discuss the concept, after which we visited Nigg to assess the potential. With its extensive waterside hard-standing dry dock, oversized sheds and deep sheltered water, Nigg certainly seemed to offer a near unique opportunity for such development.

Events moved quickly. I had a meeting to outline ideas with Stewart Stevenson MSP, then Transport Minister, who expressed interest in the superior capital and operating cost characteristics of *Pentalina*. He instructed civil servants to maintain ongoing dialogue to aid the review of ferry services that was then commencing. A subcommittee of the

Highland Council SNP Group was then set up to consider how the establishment of shipbuilding in the Cromarty Firth could be taken forward.

It was noted that if ferry policy changed for the better, there was likely to be a steady demand for some 20 fuel-efficient, medium-speed catamaran vehicle ferries in Scotland, with additional export possibilities, and that the falling pound may aid the revival of shipbuilding in Scotland. With diversification into other types of vessel a potential for £1 billion of business over approximately ten years with perhaps 400–600 direct jobs was estimated. Total start-up costs for the yard were estimated at around £30 million.

At the September Hong Kong Interferry conference, Alf Baird had made contact with a number of ferry-building yards, particularly in Australia, where Stuart Ballantyne, CEO of Sea Transport Corporation, the world's leading designers of medium-speed ferries (and designer of *Pentalina*) was interested in pulling together a consortium to set up a shipbuilding capability at Nigg. This was subject to resolution of a number of issues, not least of which was the opportunity to meet with key players in Scotland. Stuart Ballantyne, as a Scotsman well familiar with the country, had already visited Nigg. He is also a ferry operator in his own right.

It was therefore resolved to facilitate a visit by Stuart Ballantyne to meet and brief ministers, civil servants, Highlands and Islands Enterprise, Highland Council officials and members, and other key players in the development of Nigg and the remodelling of Scotland's ferry services.

Snow was lying by the time Stuart arrived – a contrast from the Australian summer of Queensland's Gold Coast. Meetings were held with the various interested parties and a visit was made to Nigg in near blizzard conditions to inspect the facilities, which were deemed ideal for the project. It was all very positive, and as discussion progressed, the idea of making a bid to operate as well as build ferries was developed.

Then came the day for the ministerial meeting. Stuart, his wife Melanie, Alf Baird and I set off on the 07.55 train from Inverness to Edinburgh. It was a cold but sunny December day. Melanie was fascinated to see the Highland landscape glistening white in its fresh winter coat. As we rolled steadily towards the capital, Stuart refined his PowerPoint presentation. In due course our little group was ushered into Stewart Stevenson's office in the Scottish Parliament building by a civil servant who remained present throughout the meeting.

It has to be said that Stuart Ballantyne is no shrinking violet. He has that Aussie 'can do' air of a swashbuckling bush ranger. He doesn't mince his words. In setting out the possibilities of assembling fuel-efficient catamarans at Nigg from imported prefabricated components, he was not slow to denounce the old-fashioned, inefficient vessels and operating methods of CalMac. He outlined how he could pull together a consortium, with the Highland Council acting as a key promoter, for the development at Nigg. He then described how his Sea Transport Corporation had been able to design, build and operate ferries at its own hand and suggested that it could do so in Scotland, in a number of cases at no subsidy, or at a lower subsidy than at present.

The minister listened to what had been said and asked a number of pertinent questions. The civil servant was uneasy.

When the meeting was over the civil servant asked me, in accusatory terms, why the presentation had deviated from the brief. I could not quite see what the problem was, other than the inclusion of possible ferry operation as well as ship assembly. But where was the harm in that? We were exploring new ways forward.

Later that day we met with Jim Mather MSP, Minister for Enterprise, Energy and Tourism, to give the same presentation. He showed interest in the economic benefit of ship assembly and wished the project well.

As we headed north again we were left with the feeling that the presentation had somehow failed to strike the right chord. That night, knowing that the civil servant would be in Nairn the following day, I emailed to arrange a meeting. The response was:

'I'm very pleased things went well with Mr Mather. Informal discussions with you have been fine in the past because you had no specific business interest to advance. Given yesterday's discussions and the fact that you are now part of a consortium that does have specific business interests it is no longer appropriate for us to have informal discussions.

'I must now treat this venture as we have treated other ventures brought to our attention. That means that while we will do nothing to hinder your venture, neither can we do anything that may benefit it. This is to protect all of our interests going forward.'

I explained that I had no financial interest in any consortium. I sought only, in consort with fellow Highland councillors, to promote ship assembly at Nigg and personally to promote more cost-effective ways of planning and running ferries in future. This cut no ice. The ongoing dialogue was terminated, although as a councillor I was permitted to participate as a stakeholder in various aspects of the Ferries Review.

With a change of administration in the council and without more active government support, the opportunity to volume assemble low-cost, state-of-the-art ferries in Scotland was lost.

THE FERRIES PLAN

In December 2012, the Scottish Government published its long awaited Ferries Plan, which was the culmination of half a decade of expensive consultation. The minister in his foreword stressed his commitment to 'delivering first class sustainable ferry services to our communities, stimulating social and economic growth across Scotland'. Within the plan there were proposals that will lead to some improvement in provision, but it was in the main a disappointment – tinkering at the edges, rather than the radical rethink that is so desperately needed.

In reality the proposals fall well short of being either first class or sustainable and will cost the taxpayer a great deal more money than is necessary. The main proposals were as follows.

Short term:
- Two vessels for Ardrossan – Arran in summer with a thrice-weekly extension to Campbeltown
- Extra winter sailings on Oban–Coll and Tiree and Barra/South Uist
- New, more frequent Small Isles passenger service plus a freight service
- Later Cumbrae and Kyles of Bute sailings
- An extra summer Colonsay sailing
- A new £42 million ferry for Stornoway (building)

Medium term:
- Free fares on the Jura (Feolin) ferry subject to transfer to Scottish Government
- A dedicated vessel to Colonsay (*Loch Nevis*)

- Increase Oban–Craignure winter frequency
- Roll out of RET for passengers and cars to most routes

Longer term (after the next tendered Clyde and Hebrides contract):
- An additional vessel for Oban–Craignure and provide a two-vessel Arran service
- Replacement vessels – four Loch-class, two medium and one large class IIA
- And for future consideration:
- Moving the Lismore vehicle ferry service to Port Appin
- Lochboisdale–Mallaig service and a new vessel thereon
- Replacement of Northern Isles vessels
- Scottish Government taking over some local authority ferries

The plan anticipated a rise in annual Scottish Government spending from £116.3 million in 2013–14 to an astonishing £180 million in 2018–19. Most disappointingly, while the consultation documents had suggested offering some individual routes to tender, in the end, the next Clyde and Hebrides contract will be tendered as a single bundle although there will be provision for the winning bidder to subcontract routes.

There were other disappointments. The ship replacement plan seemed to assume more or less the same outmoded high-cost vessel types as are employed at present. As an example, the anticipated capital cost for a new vessel for Lochboisdale–Mallaig is stated as between £20m and £40m; this is bearing in mind that *Pentalina* cost £7m and an equivalent vessel could be sourced for not much more today.

There was otherwise no consideration of any of the opportunities for route shortening that could bring immense benefits and cost savings to both taxpayer and users. Nor did the plan say much about how scheduling might be arranged to improve connectivity and permit as many useful journey opportunities as possible.

Mention was made in the plan of 'model service profiles'. It is not clear how these profiles were used in planning future development. One puzzling statement was that the existing Uig–Lochmaddy and Uig–Tarbert (Harris) services matched their service profiles. In practice, the scheduling of these services is particularly unhelpful to both traveller and haulier, and the per capita propensity to travel is very low. It is difficult to see, therefore, how these services 'match the model service profiles' whatever they are.

Bearing in mind the research undertaken by Pedersen Consulting in partnership with Napier University on CO_2 emissions and submitted to Transport Scotland, it was with some incredulity that one read the statement in para 7.4 of the plan: 'No route-specific environmental problems were identified from the operation of the ferry services covered by the Draft Ferries Plan.'

This extraordinary statement came from the Strategic Environmental Assessment (SEA) commissioned by Transport Scotland. In broad terms the report opined than there would be the potential for increased emissions from increased car traffic taking advantage of RET and increased vessel movements and number of vessels. Suggested mitigation measures included better public transport integration and more fuel-efficient vessels. These sweeping generalities were unsupported by any comparative measurement of CO_2 and other emissions attributable to ships and road vehicles and in particular to different combinations of sea and road route lengths. Without such measurement no credible conclusions can be drawn.

The SEA took no account whatsoever of the fact that ferries typically emit some *ten times* the CO_2 per passenger or car compared with road vehicles. Nor did they examine the principle of replacing long routes with short crossings and road links to yield considerable reductions in greenhouse gas emissions.

There was another extraordinary statement in the Ferries Plan: 'We will strengthen and augment existing routes rather than start up new routes. We need to recognise that we have in place a mature network of long-established routes. To introduce a new route we will need to be sure that the additional benefits to a community outweigh the substantial set-up costs of a new route.'

Of course the last sentence goes without saying, but what does not seem to be understood is that in several cases so-called 'mature' routes are chronically uneconomic. Replacement by shorter, more frequent, less polluting and cheaper-to-operate crossings would more than justify their set-up costs. Indeed, over the last few decades, as previously noted, numerous traditional (i.e. 'mature') long Scottish routes have been replaced by more efficient methods. Further overseas examples will be given in the next chapter.

A Vicious Circle of Inertia

Scotland is blessed with some good and efficient ferry operators that provide exemplary service to their communities at reasonable prices, at no cost to the taxpayer and with minimum adverse environmental impact.

On the other hand the performance of the state-funded ferry sector is well short of best practice worldwide, is both hugely costly to the public purse and to the environment, and yet poor in providing the quality of connections that our communities need.

The status quo is inefficient, costly, unsustainable and not fit for purpose. The only way costs can be brought down to more sustainable levels is by radical change to the modus operandi of our ferry connections and by market testing.

The private sector is capable of introducing more frequent and cost-effective ferry services of much superior productivity than those from the state-funded sector. They have demonstrated the ability to do this on a wholly commercial basis without capital or operating subsidy, even in the face of heavily subsidised state-owned competitors, and have been able to create new and growing business to the benefit of the communities served. Yet, rather than being embraced and rewarded for their initiative, they are discriminated against.

This phenomenon highlights serious deficiencies in the current ferry-tendering system. If, as is currently proposed, 'single-bundle' tendering is to go ahead, it would be disastrous if bidders were required to operate the current routes to the current schedules with the current ships using the same crews under the same terms and conditions and applying the same scale of charges. The opportunity for innovation would then to all intents and purposes be eliminated.

The tender process is so complex and expensive to comply with, however, that few operators have the resources to bid, thereby disadvantaging smaller operators who may be able to provide the most cost-effective solution on single routes. The upshot of recent tendering, has been considerable additional expense in terms of public funds, no real improvement in performance and little incentive to innovate. The big danger is that this will happen again with subsidies reaching such levels as to be a drain on national resources.

The main reasons for this state of affairs are:

- Old-fashioned ships of poor payload/cost characteristics (even with new tonnage)
- Poor environmental performance
- Poor track record in estimating capital and operating costs
- Selection of long, infrequent (mature) routes
- Low vehicle and passenger capacity utilisation on ships
- Large crews due to over-provision of passenger capacity
- Limited vessel utilisation due to restricted live-on-board crew hours
- Unusually generous personnel pay and conditions
- Tendering the West Coast and Northern Isles routes as single bundles
- Lack of transparency over costs and traffic figures
- Well-funded lobbying to promote the status quo to stakeholders

It is the cumulative effect of these shortcomings that has resulted in the very high subsidy levels now being paid to maintain this monolithic structure, thereby inhibiting the introduction of the kinds of ferry connections that will better and more cost-effectively serve the needs of our island and peninsular communities.

One of the fundamental shortcomings of the consultation process was the lack of meaningful route-by-route financial and statistical data. This failing made it difficult for the public to make informed judgements as to the effectiveness or otherwise of present arrangements. Nor did the consultation offer any costed alternatives with anticipated traffic generation, thus further reducing the ability of the public to judge between current and future options. Bearing in mind the considerable cost of the Ferry Review process, these are very serious shortcomings.

Overcoming these multiple deficiencies in the way Scottish state-subsidised ferries are administered, funded and operated requires a more radical approach. To address the matter of alternative options for Scottish ferry operations, Chapter 4 considers what lessons can be learned from best practice in other countries. Chapter 5 will then consider how Scottish ferries might be run more effectively.

CHAPTER 4

SOME LESSONS FROM AROUND THE WORLD

The opportunity to study ferry operations worldwide over several decades has been a great privilege. It is through such experience that yardsticks can be created to judge the performance of Scottish ferries.

In pondering the scope of what might be described, my mind turns to case upon case from near and far from which some lesson or another may be drawn.

I am reminded of the fast passenger ferry services on the Solent provided by WightLink and Red Funnel that surpass anything offered in Scotland and where one senior executive remarked: 'The CalMac people came; they looked, but they did not see.'

Then there is the amazing fleet of some 30 'Cacilheiros' ferries of the Transtejo fleet that carry about 100,000 passengers daily between Lisbon and the south bank of the Tejo – almost twice the number that travel between Oban and Barra and South Uist in a whole year. Even this is overshadowed by Hong Kong's Star Ferries' 100 million passengers annually.

Or the cheap fares of, for example, $10.55 to take a small car on the hour -long trip across the Puget Sound between Seattle and Bremerton on one of the 23 vessels of the Washington State Ferries fleet that carry 23 million passengers and 10 million vehicles per year on 9 routes with an average farebox recovery of over 70 per cent. The largest of these ferries can carry 2,500 passengers and 220 cars.

The contrast between American efficiency and Third World adaptability can be stark and each in their own way inspiring. This was brought home to me on a journey lasting several hours on the roof of a rickety, overcrowded, ex-Soviet hydrofoil at the turn of the millennium on Cambodia's Tonle Sap River and Lake. While a health and safety nightmare in Western terms, the 'can do' attitude demonstrated the creativity and resilience of the human spirit of a plucky nation just recovering from the horrors of the Pol Pot genocide.

To do justice to a comparative evaluation of world ferries would fill several large volumes and that is not attempted here. I have instead focussed on three geographical areas – Norway, British Columbia and Australia/New Zealand – each of which offers insights into how a better future may be secured for Scottish ferry services.

THE NORSE WAY

Once one of the poorest nations in Europe, Norway (population five million) is now one of the world's wealthiest. With a per capita gross national income twice that of the UK, Norway stashed its oil revenues to create a massive $600 billion sovereign fund, while the UK squandered its oil income. For those and other reasons Norway is often portrayed as the kind of country an independent Scotland could be.

Since the 1960s Norway's efficient ferry system too has been seen by many as offering a model for improving island communications in Scotland in a cost-effective manner. As described earlier, the Highland Transport Board recommended the adoption of Norwegian methods and the former Zetland County Council (later Shetland Islands Council) and Western Ferries put this into practice to the great benefit of the communities served by them. Sadly their example was not followed by the state-funded sector, with resulting inadequate service coupled with massive subsidies.

What is so special about the way the Norwegians do things?

Ancestral Connections

First I should declare an interest. My grandfather Captain Peder Thorwald Pedersen was a Norwegian master mariner, who settled initially in Liverpool and then in Ardrossan, Ayrshire where my father and I were born. My own childhood was spent among boats and ships at Aberdeen where I spent most of my youth, and the Clyde where I spent much of my summer holidays. A very Scottish experience, but all the while some hazy sense of Norwegian maritime heritage lurked in the family tradition.

That Norwegian maritime heritage came into focus for me in April 1977 when, at the instigation of the HIDB, I went on a five-day study visit to Norway; outward by chartered light plane from Inverness to Vigra (Ålesund) where fish processing was the object of interest. From thence I travelled by bus to Vestnes and ferry to Molde to spend an afternoon and morning at the headquarters of the legendary regional ferry company Møre og Romsdal Fylkesbåter (MRF). There, Stein Blindheim, the company's *sous-chef* provided a wealth of data. From Molde I proceeded by bus and ferry to Åndalsnes and then by train to Oslo, where I had the free use of a flat. In Oslo, the transport minister was kind enough to fill me in on the Norwegian government policy background. From Oslo I travelled to Stavanger by sleeper train to meet up with the operations director of the forward-thinking ferry company Stavangerske D/S. From there I returned to Aberdeen by getting a free lift on a Loganair oil charter plane (one could do that in those days) and on to Inverness by train. I believe I was the only member of HIDB staff to make a Norway trip under budget and to return a proportion of the imprest provided for my expenses.

This had been my first time in the land of my ancestors and I was smitten. Norway had been a real eye-opener. As an aid to further research, I determined to learn Norwegian. To this end a dozen or so of us created a self-help Norwegian class meeting consecutively in each other's houses. In due course by this means we all passed our Higher Norwegian exams. The group ultimately developed into the Highland Scandinavian Association. Of more relevance to the subject in hand, I resolved to undertake a full and ongoing analysis of my researches into Norwegian ferry operations and policy.

Norwegian Coastal Shipping

Norway's vigorous seaborne Viking past is well known. By the fourteenth century, however, this vigour had evaporated, partly due to competition from the Hanseatic League and partly as a result of the Black Death. In 1380 Norway was absorbed into a union with Denmark that lasted over four centuries. In 1814, against the wishes of the people, Norway was ceded to Sweden but under a new constitution that guaranteed a large measure of autonomy. Full independence from Sweden was secured in 1905. Norway is nowadays a member of NATO but not of the European Union.

With an area half as large again as the United Kingdom, Norway's extreme geography features steep and high mountains and a 25,000km coastline deeply indented by fjords and fringed by numerous islands. Because of this, until modern times, overland travel was very difficult in much of the country, especially in the west, where perforce the sea was the main highway. A variety of traditional craft undertook the movement of goods and people between the scattered coastal settlements and the main centres.

Scheduled passenger, goods and mail steam navigation became established on the Norwegian coast during the second half of the nineteenth century. Before long, a complex series of local multi-port steamer networks evolved linking the main commercial centres such as Oslo, Stavanger, Bergen, Ålesund and Trondheim with their respective rural hinterlands of fjord-side and island communities. In 1893 in response to government concern that northern Norway remained outside the regular steamer networks, Captain Richard With in his vessel *Vesterålen* inaugurated a new passenger, cargo and mail steamer route from Trondheim to Hammerfest, calling at eleven intermediate ports. This was the first *Hurtigruten* or coastal express route. Before long, other operators joined the coastal express, which was extended southward to Bergen in 1898 (thrice weekly) and northwards to Kirkenes, near the Russian border, in 1908. By 1936 daily sailings were provided by 14 ships.

By 1900, Bergen had emerged as the predominant commercial centre fielding by far the largest merchant fleet, and one predominantly of steamers. This dominance was further enhanced by the opening of the Bergen–Oslo railway in 1909. By this time, too, Norway's merchant fleet was the world's fourth largest.

For decades, the pattern of local fjord and long-distance express steamer services continued as the scattered coastal communities' main lifeline with the outside world where the steamer call was the highlight of the day. Mike Bent's superb *Steamers of the Fjords* and *Coastal Express*, give the English-speaking reader detailed insights into the development of these services and their socio-economic setting. Some measure of the scale of service may be gleaned from the fact that, on a typical summer Saturday in the early 1930s, there were no fewer than 94 local steamer departures from Bergen's Vågen and Nøstet, each to a different destination. That this was so was largely due to the lack of roads in western Norway. Of the quarter million inhabitants in Bergen's hinterland of Sogn og Fjordane and Hordaland in 1929, only 11 per cent had a continuous road connection. But change was in the air.

Early Vehicle Ferry Development

It was in those inter-war years that the first tentative car ferry services commenced. These generally utilised adapted motor vessels whose foredeck was cleared to carry a few vehicles. In 1929 Møre og Romsdal's roads department announced a plan to eliminate a number of fjord steamer routes by expanding the area's road network and creating vehicle ferry links to 'bridge' the gaps where sea intervened. The Danes pioneered the now characteristic Scandinavian 'lock-on' end-loading RO-RO concept, but it was not until the 1930s that the first true RO-RO ferry was in operation in the Norwegian fjords. She was *Geiranger*, with a capacity for 17 cars, constructed for service in Møre og Romsdal. By 1939, several further RO-RO ferries, supplemented by a range of side-loaders, were in operation in the western fylker (counties) of Rogaland, Hordaland, Sogn og Fjordane and Møre og Romsdal, and across Oslofjord between Moss and Horten. Quite a number of routes were of considerable length, as up to this point new road construction had been limited. Nevertheless it was now possible to drive, using ferries, between a number of important, and many minor, settlements whereas a decade before that could not be done.

The traumatic German wartime occupation of Norway slowed vehicle ferry development for the duration. It was a case of making do with what was available after vessels had been requisitioned, or lost, more often than not as a result of Allied attack. On the other hand, some new, strategically important roads were built by the Axis administration to aid the movement of Wehrmacht troops.

The immediate post-war period featured shortages of materials coupled with reinstatement of war damage. In the 1950s and 60s, however, a progressive expansion of the road networks in the west and a rapid increase in car ownership saw substantial investment in RO-RO ferries with a resultant exponential increase in vehicular traffic on the ferries. The table below illustrates the rate of growth in Møre og Romsdal at that time.

Year	Vehicles	Passengers
1938	27,825	275,343
1950	82,734	823,257
1960	448,794	2,465,732

This pattern was replicated throughout Norway with car, bus, truck and vehicle ferries replacing traditional fjord steamer services.

In some fylker during this period, ferry operations were run on a commercial basis, charging what the market could bear. In Møre og Romsdal, however, as part of the traffic plan of 1953, it was considered that as ferries acted as 'floating bridges', charges should be no greater than the cost of driving the equivalent distance by road. As a consequence, a subsidised scale of charges was put in place. Such was the success of this scheme that in 1959 the government selected Møre og Romsdal to trial a more systematic approach to vehicle ferry operations with a view to applying them to the country as a whole.

The MRF Report

Leader in the process of systematisation was Mr K.H. Oppegård, chief roads surveyor of the fylke of Møre og Romsdal who, as previously noted, subsequently advised the Highland Transport Board and Zetland County Council. In 1961, Mr Oppegård was elected chair of a committee of three tasked with undertaking the in-depth analysis of the principles of ferry operations. The report was a masterpiece of clear scientific analysis of ferry economics and operations in thorough systematic detail, with the emphasis throughout on cost-effectiveness.

As already alluded to with reference to the work of the Highland Transport Board, the key principles set out in the report were:

- Adoption of the shortest practicable sea crossing
- As a result, minimise costs and maximise frequency
- Efficient standardised vessel designs and terminals to aid interchangeability
- Where possible employ shore-based crews in shifts

These key principles were confirmed only after meticulous analysis of crewing tasks; capital and running cost structures and variables;

power-to-speed ratios and costs; maintenance; engine installations; propulsion; capacity and utilisation; single- and double-ended ferries relative to route length; traffic peaks and troughs; passenger comfort and catering; deck layout; proposed standard ferries; terminal design; link-spans and mooring; automated terminals; traffic flow; traffic growth prognosis and much more.

The report, whose Norwegian title is *Ferjeutvalget I Møre og Roms-dal, Innstilling av 15 desember 1963*, was published by Møre og Romsdal Fylkesbåtar and presented to the Norwegian Storting (parliament) in 1964 to become the foundation on which Norwegian ferry policy has been developed subsequently.

Just over a decade later I visited the offices of Møre og Romsdal Fylkesbåtar. Their approach was so refreshing I arranged on return-ing to Scotland to have the report translated under the English title *The MRF Report*. The translation was undertaken at modest cost by Anna Kristin Stoknes, the young daughter of our Norwegian teacher, herself from Møre og Romsdal, and edited by myself. The quality of the translation of this magnum opus by a schoolgirl is if anything even more impressive than the original report. Copies were sent to the Scottish Office to little apparent avail.

What also struck me about the set-up at MRF was the comprehen-siveness of the company's annual reports. In contrast to the tendency to obfuscation of the David MacBrayne Group reports, the MRF reports set out clear detail on route-by-route traffic, revenue and costs statis-tics. The ship-by-ship costs are broken down to such detail as overtime, pensions, fuel, lubrication oil, auxiliaries, telephone and radio, etc. It was considered right and proper that such information should be provided as the ferry operation was subsidised by taxpayers' money. One could not but agree.

State Ferry Policy

The Norwegian government went along with the MRF report and acknowledged that 'state-granted road ferries', as they are defined, are regarded as an integral part of the road system. This fits with the Norwegian government's policy aim of retention of population in the more rural parts of the country by encouraging economic development and good social provision. Good road transport and cheap, frequent ferry connections were seen as fundamental components in this policy.

The standardised terminals, as part of the road network, are now owned by the state.

A national scale of charges was introduced in 1968 which resulted in a substantial reduction of fares on most services although the new tariff was not as cheap as had been in force with MRF, where fares rose. Nationally there was a leap in ferry traffic, especially in terms of winter usage. The national tariff is based on two elements – the passage distance (zone) and vehicle length. Fares on routes of, say, 10km are the same wherever in the country they are. The relatively low level of fares means that in most cases they do not cover running costs. The difference is covered by subsidy.

A set of standardised ferry designs were adopted, of which the double-ended *pendleferje* (shuttle ferry) of various sizes has become almost universal.

At the time of my visit to MRF, there were 170 ferry routes operated by 255 vehicle ferries carrying almost 12 million vehicles and almost 38 million passengers. Although in recent years many ferry services have been replaced by fixed links (bridges, causeways or tunnels), there are still in total 160 ferry vessels, with a combined capacity of some 9,000 PCUs (passenger car equivalent units), operated by 18 different companies on 124 routes, or 'connections' (*forbindelsen* in Norwegian, signifying 'binding together'). Connections (routes) vary in length from 0.6km to 113km.

In recent years new and improved standards have been laid down for different categories of route. Busy trunk routes are open round the clock. Through regional routes should be frequent, usually half hourly, and open at least 18 hours per day with 97 per cent of vehicles shipped on the departure desired. Local connections may be to a lesser standard.

In setting these standards the state purchases the service from each ferry operator under a ten-year contract, negotiable each year. The contracting arrangement, which is considered to have worked well, is now under review. Recent total financial outcomes are as follows:

	£ million
Total operating cost	164
Revenue	90
State grant	74

Operating costs are kept under tight review and are made available publicly in detail on an operator-by-operator, route-by-route basis.

Hurtigbåter

While the traditional fjord steamer is but a memory, its place has been taken in numerous instances by *hurtigbåter* (high-speed passenger boats), also known as *snøggbåter*.

The Norwegians pioneered fast passenger craft designs in the 1960s and 70s, initially using hydrofoils. It was however the Westamaran catamaran designed by Westermoen of Mandal in 1973 that replaced the hydrofoils and brought about a revolution in passenger ferry design and operation. Catamarans with excellent seakeeping characteristics now predominate on most of the numerous fast passenger services. These vary from the intercity Flaggruten Stavanger–Haugesund–Bergen route to numerous stopping services linking fjord-side and island communities with their regional centres, almost in the time honoured way except much faster and more frequently. When in the old days a return trip to, say, Bergen might have involved two long overnight journeys, it is now possible by bus and *hurtigbåt* to commute daily or to have ample time for business or shopping in either direction. Naturally, because of the useful journey opportunities now possible, the traffic carried by these services is immeasurably greater than in former times and outlying communities have been revitalised.

Hurtigruten

The daily traditional Hurtigruten Coastal Express Route between Bergen and Kirkenes continues to provide what is claimed, with justification, to be 'the world's most beautiful sea voyage'. The round trip takes 12 days, with 34 ports of call undertaken by a fleet of 12 vessels, all now operated by a single company, Hurtigruten ASA. With the huge improvements in road and air transport, the service is no longer quite the lifeline it once was. From the 1980s, operating subsidies were reduced and the emphasis changed to tourism. New, bigger and more luxurious ships were introduced, with hot tubs, bars, restaurants and other amenities. Nevertheless, Hurtigruten still provides a useful passenger and cargo service, and operates 365 days a year.

Hutrigruten ASA also operates cruises to Greenland, South America and Antarctica, as well as local ferries and high-speed regional express boats in Norway.

BEAUTIFUL BRITISH COLUMBIA

With its island-strewn, deeply indented coastline, this rugged mountainous Pacific province covers seven times the area of the UK with a
population a little less than that of Scotland at 4.6 million. It might be
described as 'Scotland on steroids'.

The Early Years

Steam navigation in the Pacific Northwest began as early as 1836 with
the little Hudson Bay steamer *Beaver*. The Fraser River gold strike of
1850 fuelled a flood of gold-hungry immigrants, served by a fleet of
mainly American steamers, so ending the Bay Company's monopoly.
In 1871 British Columbia joined the Canadian Confederation on the
promise of a transcontinental railway link to the rest of Canada. One of
the advocates of the railway was BC's legendary second premier: a Nova
Scotian, who changed his name from the prosaic William Alexander
Smith to Amor de Cosmos ('Lover of the Universe').

And so by 1886, the metals of the Canadian Pacific Railway had crossed
the Rockies to terminate first at Port Moody, then a year later at a place
further west on the south shore of Burrard Inlet. There wasn't much
there at the time by way of human presence – a few Indians, loggers and
sawmills. There was, however, the 6,000 acres of prime waterfront land
demanded by the CPR's formidable William Cornelius Van Horne and
given away by BC's fawning seventh premier William Smythe. The deep
water adjacent to the railway terminal was ideal to develop a sheltered
harbour with ready access to the Pacific. To the landward, a settlement
materialised. It was named Vancouver, now Canada's third largest city.

As a transcontinental railhead, it was inevitable that Vancouver would
become a major shipping hub. The CPR immediately established its
own trans-Pacific Royal Mail shipping operation to Japan and China,
featuring the famous 'Empress' liners, while the Union Steamship
Company of British Columbia Ltd was formed in 1889 to serve the
coastal settlements and canneries of the north-west. At that time too,
small steam ferries designed to carry passengers, cattle and horse-
drawn vehicles on the roll-on/roll-off principle commenced operation
across the Burrard Inlet.

As Victoria, the provincial capital, and the growing city of Nanaimo
were located offshore on Vancouver Island, regular steamer connections

with the mainland were clearly essential. Amor de Cosmos, by this time a Victoria newspaper proprietor, proposed a short rail-linked crossing between Swartz Bay and English Bluffs near Tsawassen, but it was to be 70 years before his visionary ideas came to fruition.

In the event, daily steamer connections on the longer passages between Vancouver and both ports were instituted. By the turn of the century, the Victoria service was deemed inadequate and the CPR took over the route. This formed the basis of the CPR's BC Coastal Services to be managed for 30 years by the redoubtable Captain James Troup. The first new ship after the takeover was *Princess Victoria*, a 20-knot, three-funnelled beauty. She arrived from Newcastle upon Tyne in 1903 to provide a vastly improved level of service on the Vancouver–Victoria route. Over the ensuing decades, additional fast and luxurious *Princess* liners served on what was known as the 'Triangle Service' linking Vancouver, Victoria and Seattle (Washington). The schedule was such that two sailings were provided in each direction between the two Canadian cities – one in daylight and the other overnight.

Shipping Automobiles

Even before the First Wold War, there was a demand to carry automobiles, and the *Princess* liners were eventually adapted to load a limited number of cars via side doors. In 1918, Canadian Pacific purchased the first seagoing RO-RO ferry specifically designed to carry cars on the BC coast. She was *Daily*, built at Tacoma, Washington in 1913 and could carry 18 cars and 100 plus passengers. She was renamed *Island Princess*. In 1923 the larger *Motor Princess* was ordered – a motor vessel able to accommodate 45 cars on two decks and to load and discharge them via bow, stern and side doors. After an initial period on the Bellingham (WA)–Sidney run, she plied between Vancouver and Nanaimo in consort with *Princess Patricia*, the former Clyde turbine steamer *Queen Alexandra*. In 1930 *Island Princess* was purchased and renamed *Cy Peck* by the new locally owned Gulf Islands Ferry Company to inaugurate an improved RO-RO service to those islands. By 1938 the Canadian Pacific BC Coastal Service shipped 63,403 automobiles. This figure was far in advance of vehicle shipments on Scottish seagoing services. It was, however, increasingly regarded locally as inadequate and certainly a pale shadow of what was to come on the BC coast in later decades.

Things started to hot up in 1951 when the Puget Sound ferry

services operated by Captain Alexander Marshal Peabody and his Black Ball Line had been bought out by the State of Washington. That year he built RO-RO terminals at Horseshoe Bay on the BC mainland and Departure Bay just outside Nanaimo, offering a much shorter, more convenient and frequent no-frills service than the longer Canadian Pacific route from Vancouver. The introduction of five return crossings daily was a great success and the Canadian Pacific took a beating.

Victoria's service from Vancouver was by now regarded as abysmal. The once highly regarded side-loading *Princesses* were now unable to cope with the number of automobiles presented for shipment and at times the only sailing available was the slow six-and-a-half-hour overnight on which sleeping accommodation regularly sold out. The company said the provision of a more direct and frequent service was neither practical nor profitable. How often have we heard that in Scotland?

BC Ferries

In 1958 a serious labour dispute involving both the Canadian Pacific and the Black Ball Line brought BC's most remarkable and colourful premier, William Andrew Cecil Bennett, into the frame. Under his robust and visionary leadership, the upshot was the creation of BC Ferries and a wholly new approach to the ferry business.

What was required to connect Victoria with the mainland was a short shuttle crossing every two hours. The announcement of the proposed location of mainland terminal was met with incredulity and ridicule. It was to be an artificial island linked by a two-mile long causeway near the Indian reserve of Tsawwassen. The terminal on the Vancouver Island side was to be sheltered Swartz Bay at the end of a bumpy dirt road. This was almost exactly the route Amor de Cosmos had recommended 70 years before – a 41km route as compared with the 140km of the CPR route. In the face of cries of 'madness', the artificial island at Tsawwassen was built together with a 7-mile highway to meet the new causeway. On Vancouver Island a new road was built from Sidney to Swartz Bay. Terminals were then constructed at both ends of the route. Two new RO-RO ships *Sidney* and *Tsawwassen* were built at North Vancouver's Burrard Dry Dock, each ship with a capacity for 138 cars at a service speed of 18 knots to undertake the passage in one hour and forty minutes. The whole operation commenced in June 1960. At a stroke total daily car carrying capacity was increased from some 200 to over 2,000.

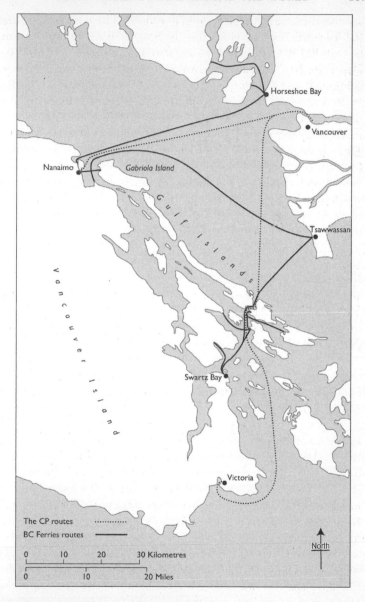

The CP routes ··············
BC Ferries routes ——————

0   10   20   30 Kilometres

0   10   20 Miles

North

BC Ferries

In the first year the service turned a profit and such was demand that two further ships were ordered, making an hourly service possible and increasing daily car-carrying capacity to 4,400. The 'mature' CPR route were outclassed by the short, frequent crossing and had to withdraw from the Vancouver–Victoria route. Air Canada was hit too, reducing its flights between the two cities from 22 a day to 6.

In 1961 BC ferries purchased the assets of Gulf Islands Ferries and the Black Ball Line. As a consequence, the company's area of operation and traffic grew rapidly. In 1966 *Queen of Prince Rupert* inaugurated the spectacular 20-hour northern route from Kelsey Bay (later Port Hardy) to Vancouver Island via the Inside Passage to Prince Rupert. Then between 1970 and 1975 BC Ferries carried out its famous 'stretch and lift' programme whereby four major vessels were cut in half so that an 84-foot midsection could be 'spliced' in, then later 'sliced' horizontally, to slide a new upper car deck into place.

The BC Ferries website www.bcferries.com has long been a model of good practice. Besides providing comprehensive travel and reservations information, amenities and current wait times at terminals, it lists much detail about the fleet, and monthly traffic statistics.

In 2003 BC Ferries was officially relaunched as a new, independent commercial company and renamed British Columbia Ferry Services Inc. which, by 2012, conveyed 20 million passengers and almost 8 million vehicles per annum through 47 ports of call on 25 routes operated by 35 vessels, the largest of which can carry 470 cars and 2,100 passengers. All in all, a remarkable achievement.

Skullduggery, Fiasco and Disaster

Like most large ferry companies, BC Ferries had had its share of mishaps, most of them relatively minor. The 1990s, however, were not a good time for the BC provincial government or for BC Ferries.

The sequence opens with the revelation that the genial finance minister Dave Stupich was found to have transferred six-figure sums from Nanaimo charities to his own account. A political diversion was required. What followed was to become the greatest catalogue of errors in BC's transport history. It was motivated by a desire to reduce congestion at the busy Horseshoe Bay and Departure Bay terminals.

First we must go back 20 years when, under the administration of Premier W.A.C. Bennett, a proposal was tabled in 1972 to build bridges from Vancouver Island over Dodd Narrows and False Narrows and a highway accross Gabriola Island to a new ferry terminal at the eastern extremity of that island. From there a ferry would run on the short 32km to Vancouver's North Arm Jetty, replacing the 54km Horseshoe Bay–Departure Bay route. Although it would have involved considerable up-front capital expenditure, the cumulative savings in operating costs and improvement in travel time would have been very substantial. When the Bennett administration fell later that year, however, the project was buried by the incoming administration partly on the grounds that it would reduce unionised ferry workers' overtime hours. Then in 1985, the removal of the highway authority from overall planning of ferry crossings further undermined the ability to plan strategically, leaving decisions primarily with 'ship' men.

Moving forward to 1994; BC's thirtieth premier, Michael Franklin Harcourt, announced the proposal to build three novel high-speed aluminium-hulled catamaran vehicle ferries capable of 37 knots for the Nanaimo–Horseshoe Bay route. As they were required to fit existing terminals they were not true catamarans. They were given the name *Pacificat* and they were to prove an utter fisaco. The first entered service in 1999, two years behind schedule. They were well over budget, unreliable, unable to cope with large commercial vehicles, and had poor passenger accommodation and voracious fuel consumption. This, coupled with hull corrosion, cracking and blocked intakes due to floating debris, rendered the concept untenable. The second vessel lased three days in service before being withdrawn and the third never entered service at all. The whole exercise had cost $463 million. The ships were eventually sold in 2003 for just under $20 million or 4 cents in the dollar!

While the *Pacificats* were being conceived, it was decided to build a new terminal at Duke Point just south of Nanaimo and from there to create a supplementary 64km ferry route to Tsawwassen, thereby relieving congestion at the existing terminals. This was of course a longer, not a shorter crossing, and therefore more expensive to operate.

There is no doubt that the *Pacificat* fiasco was a wake-up call for BC Ferries, as admitted to me by Craig Elder, the company's Head of Strategy and Corporate Planning when I visited him in Victoria in 2001. Henceforth the policy was to be fiscally responsible evolution rather than revolution and to leave catamaran design to the Australians who 'know how to make them properly'.

A few years later, in 2006, as I had never previously travelled BC's famed Inside Passage, I planned a trip to put that right. Having booked accommodation for the various stages of the journey, including the Alaska Marine Highway from Prince Rupert to Skagway, I could not understand why the otherwise excellent BC Ferries website would not allow me to make a reservation, nor could I get through on the telephone. As it happens, my cousin June and her husband George live on Gabriola Island. I phoned to see if they could help.

'Oh,' said George; 'The ship sank.'

And that is how I discovered that the 8,806 gross ton BC Ferries flagship *Queen of the North* rammed Gil Island at full speed. She sank within an hour with the loss of two lives.

In the absence of normal booking facilities, I phoned the BC Ferries corporate HQ in Victoria, first to offer my sympathies and secondly ascertain that the *Queen of Prince Rupert* had been drafted in to operate a restricted schedule on the Inside Passage alternating with her normal Queen Charlotte Islands duties. In the event, with a little juggling of accommodation plans, passage was booked for what transpired to be a memorable trip in excellent company. There was of course much lurid speculation on board as to what had happened on the fateful night the *Queen of the North* had gone down, much of which it would be improper to report here.

Exactly a year after the sinking, BC Ferries released the results of its investigation and blamed the accident on human error caused by three crew members, specifically the *Queen of the North's* helmswoman, and the ship's second and fourth officers who were in charge of navigation.

Better Times

For a world-leading ferry company that brought such radical and beneficial improvement to island life, it is sad and not a little unfair that BC Ferries suffered so much misfortune over that decade and a half. Notwithstanding these setbacks, I have met with nothing but courtesy and openness from the company's staff and it is to be hoped that while there are lessons to be learned, the memory of these unfortunate events will recede and that a bright future awaits BC Ferries and the enterprising folk of beautiful British Columbia.

ANTIPODEAN CATAMARANS

By sea round the Cape of Good Hope came Australia's European settlers (willing and unwilling) and manufactured goods. By sea round Cape Horn went her exports of wool, grain, gold and those who had struck it rich returning to flaunt their wealth. Sailing ships dominated those trades later than elsewhere. In fact by the 1930s, the grain trade from Australia to Europe was the last enterprise in which big square-riggers could engage with any profit.

Sail also long dominated the Australian coastal trade as exemplified by South Australia's mosquito fleet of small coasting ships. These cutters, ketches, schooners and brigantines traded with the remote coastal communities at a period when roads barely existed. The last of the mosquito fleet were withdrawn from service in 1982.

The first steamship in Australian waters was the *Sophia Jane* which arrived in Australia in 1834, and by 1841 the P.S. *Shamrock* and P.S. *Sovereign* provided a fortnightly Melbourne–Sydney–Brisbane service. From that time coastal passenger steamers – a high proportion of them Scottish-built – provided the main means of transport between the colonial communities, even well after federation in 1901 and the emergence of intercity rail travel. It was the development of regular air services and the rising costs of steamship operation after the Second World War that led to the demise of most coastal passenger services.

From the above it may be thought that Australia was destined to be behind the times. This is far from being the case. Australia is now the world leader in catamaran ferry design, construction and operation.

Aussie Cats

The principle of the twin-hulled catamaran is not new. From about 1500 BC Polynesian navigators had been able to make ocean voyages of thousands of miles using outrigger and twin-hulled canoes. Their feats of navigation are astonishing, and by AD 1200 their reach stretched from Taiwan in the north to New Zealand in the south and from Madagascar through the South Seas, possibly even to South America.

The advantage of the catamaran is that a pair of narrow hulls spaced apart and joined together by struts or a deck, moves more easily and speedily through the water than a beamy single (mono) hull, while also providing a broad and stable platform to carry a payload. For these reasons the catamaran has become increasingly adopted by ferry operators.

As has already been noted, the Norwegian firm of Westermoen pioneered the volume production of efficient high-speed passenger catamarans in the mid 1970s. It was the Australians, however, who developed the concept further with a wide range of new applications including large vehicle-carrying catamarans that have found worldwide markets. Three important players are now described.

International Catamarans (The Incat group) evolved from local boat-building and operating companies in Hobart, Tasmania, to specialise in the construction of fast ferries in aluminium. In 1983 the 'wave-piercing' design was conceived; the 8.7-metre prototype craft *Little Devil* first underwent trials in 1984, followed in 1985 by the 28-metre wave-piercing catamaran, *Spirit of Victoria*. The current range of waterjet-propelled catamarans still follow this wave-piercing design.

In 1988 a contract was signed for the construction of a car-carrying passenger catamaran for Sealink British Ferries. The 74-metre vessel emerged in 1990 as *Hoverspeed Great Britain* and on her delivery voyage she won the Hales Trophy for the fastest transatlantic crossing by a commercial passenger ship, smashing the existing record by 3 hours and 14 minutes. In 1992, the 74-metre *SeaCat Scotland* was delivered to Sea Containers. She was employed briefly between Dover and Calais prior to inaugurating the new 90-minute Stranraer–Belfast service – the first Scottish high-speed car-carrying service and indeed the first across the Irish Sea.

The transatlantic record was broken again in 1998 by the Incat 91-metre *Express* on her delivery voyage. While en route between Manhattan and Tariffa, Spain, her average speed was 38.88 knots. In so doing, she was the first passenger ship to cover more than 1,000 miles in 24 hours (1,018 nautical miles, in fact). *Express* is now operating for P&O Ferries between Larne, Cairnryan and Troon.

By 2007 Incat had built almost 40 per cent of the world's high-speed vehicle-passenger ferry fleet over 50 metres in length.

Austal, Incat's main competitor, commenced operations at Henderson near Fremantle in Western Australia in 1988 building catamaran and mono-hull vessels in aluminium for the international market. Today, with shipyards in Western Australia, the United States of America and the Philippines, Austal has delivered more than 220 vessels for customers around the world. The product range includes passenger and vehicle-passenger ferries, luxury yachts and, as a major global defence prime contractor, military vessels.

Apparently Austal had offered Caledonian MacBrayne a very competitive medium-speed, vehicle-carrying catamaran design, with performance and cost characteristics far superior to any vessel operated by the Scottish company then or since, but were brushed aside.

The Sea Transport Corporation is a family concern based on Queensland's Gold Coast that owns, operates and constructs commercial vessels and offers specialist marine design and consulting services. It was founded in 1976 by the swashbuckling Stuart Ballantyne and has a wide range of successful, innovative craft now operating in 45 countries worldwide, including Pentland Ferries groundbreaking medium-speed catamaran *Pentalina*. The company also supplies pre-cut 'kit' vessels allowing builders to begin construction immediately and to reduce overall construction time.

Some years before I met Stuart in connection with the design and construction of Pentland Ferries' *Pentalina*, I had heard of him, while visiting ferry operators in Australia, as designer of the catamaran vehicle ferries operating between the Bellarine and Mornington Peninsulas in Victoria, and on the Kangaroo Island service in South Australia.

In 2010, the company was commissioned to build ten 50-metre medium-speed (16-knot) roPax catamarans for the Philippines, a design which would be readily adaptable to service in Scotland.

Australian Catamaran Operators
As the three examples above illustrate, the Aussies are master builders and marketers of catamarans. The same is true of operating twin-hulled vessels of all shapes, sizes and speeds. They are to be found virtually anywhere there is marine activity around the continent's coasts – nowhere more so than in the case of Sydney Harbour's famous ferry fleet of 28 passenger ferries carrying 14 million passengers annually. A high proportion of the fleet are cats, including the nine 400-passenger, 12-knot 'First Fleet' class working the Inner Harbour; the 22-knot,

'low wash' 230 passenger 'River Cats' running up the Parramatta River; and the 26-knot, 250-passenger 'Super Cats' running to the eastern suburbs. As this scale of passenger-only operation is of a wholly different order of magnitude from that obtaining in Scotland, it is worth looking at a couple of examples that may be more instructive.

Kangaroo Island lies on the edge of the windy and fearsome Great Southern Ocean. It is Australia's third largest island and has a population of around 4,300. The closest point on the South Australian mainland is Cape Jervis at 8 miles (13km) distant.

Once again this is the story of a long, infrequent, 'mature' route superseded by a short, frequent one. From 1907 to 1961 the Gulf Steamship Company (from 1915 renamed Coast Steamships Ltd) operated the Greenock-built passenger/cargo steamship *Karatta* as the main carrier on the 75-mile (120km) route between Port Adelaide and Kingscote, Kangaroo Island's capital.

Following *Karatta*'s withdrawal from service, the RO-RO ferry MV *Troubridge* operated the route, followed in turn in 1987 by the severely criticised *Island Seaway*. A much shorter and more frequent passenger service had been inaugurated, however, in the early 1970s by Kangaroo Island businessman Peter March, a move which ultimately killed the long route. His 'Philanderer Ferries' pioneered the short twelve-mile (19km) crossing from the mainland port of Cape Jervis to Penneshaw, the nearest port on Kangaroo Island. His *Philanderer 3* was the first passenger- and vehicle-carrying vessel on the short route – a catamaran designed by Stuart Ballantyne. In 1989 the operation was acquired by Kangaroo Island SeaLink who, under various owners, have run the route since that time.

The company operates two catamaran ferries: the 16-knot, 55-car, 353-passenger *Sealion 2000* and the 17.8-knot, 53-car, 244-passenger *Spirit of Kangaroo Island* on the 45-minute crossing with coach connections between Adelaide and Kingscote. So well suited are the vessels to the crossing that SeaLink's cancellation rate due to extreme weather, sea conditions or breakdown is less than 0.5 per cent. Ferries operate a minimum of two return trips per day, with one vessel and up to nine services per day during peak periods with both vessels. Each vessel's 2.2 MW of engine power has a fuel consumption of some 450 litres per hour; half that of an equivalent conventional CalMac Class IIA ferry. SeaLink is now the main driver of tourism to and from Kangaroo Island, opening the island to the international market.

Brisbane Ferry Network features a fast, frequent river bus service with a fleet of 19 catamarans known as CityCats criss-crossing a network of 24 terminals stretching along the Brisbane River from the University of Queensland at St Lucia to Northshore Hamilton. CityCats operate every 15 minutes for most of the day, with express routes and more frequent services during peak times. The concept is reminiscent of the Glasgow Cluthas (river buses) of the late nineteenth century. In addition to the CityCat service, nine cross-river mono-hull 8- to 12-knot CityFerries with passenger capacities varying between 54 and 80, are also operated as part of the network.

Prior to 1991 the CityFerries had been operated directly by Brisbane City Council. In that year, River Connections took over their operation and maintenance and in 1996 launched the fast CityCat river bus service with four specially built catamarans, each capable of carrying 149 passengers. In response to strong growth in CityCat patronage, the CityCat fleet was augmented over the next few years, bringing the total fleet to eight.

I was privileged to meet up with Lyle White and Sunny Newitt who showed me round the Hawthorne maintenance depot and who explained the CityCat design philosophy of speed, economy, quietness and ability to stop. The shallow-draft, low-wash hull forms – similar to the Sydney–Parramatta catamarans – allow the vessels to travel at 22 knots along the urban river without causing discomfort to other river users. The hull form also reduced the need for a large power output, such that fuel consumption is around 50 litres of ultra-low sulphur diesel per hour. Engine insulation reduces noise to not more than 65dB, well within acceptable levels, and by fitting bakes to the propeller shafts, the boats, with their large bladed propellers acting as water brakes, are able to stop within their own length from full speed.

In 2003, Brisbane City Council transferred the contract to TransdevTSL Brisbane Ferries (a joint venture) to operate CityCat and Cityferry services and from 2004, 'second generation' CityCats have been introduced and the network restructured to include more late-night services. These developments brought a huge increase in passenger numbers.

Under normal circumstances, the Brisbane Ferry Network achieves 99 per cent on-time running. The most abnormal circumstance experienced by the Network, however, was the devastating 2011 flood, as a result of which, all CityCat and ferry terminals sustained damage. The full service was restored within 90 days.

Kiwi Cats

When road and rail communications were rudimentary, coastal steamships provided New Zealand's main means of connecting the growing coastal communities with each other. There were the elegant, Scottish-built, green-hulled ships of the Union Steamship Company of New Zealand Ltd, sporting the same orangey-red funnel with black ring-stays as the Cunard Line, Isle of Man Steam Packet Company and of David MacBrayne of old. This iconic colouring was introduced by the legendary Scottish engineer Robert Napier. The services covered by the Union ships were extensive, serving the numerous ports and inlets on the Kiwi coast, including the famed Wellington–Lyttleton ferry linking the North and South Islands nightly. The Union Company also linked New Zealand across the Tasman Sea with Sydney in New South Wales, across the Pacific with the far-flung South Sea Islands and Vancouver as part of the "All Red" route (i.e., transiting entirely through the territories of the British Empire) between the UK and the Antipodes.

Each of these icons of New Zealand's shipping heritage has been swept away by a modern road system, air transport and, in the case of the old Auckland ferries, by the Auckland Harbour Bridge. Yet, there is a new vibrancy in the Dominion's coastal waters. North and South Islands are linked across the Cook Straight by modern RO-RO passenger, vehicle and train ferries.

As with Australia, passenger- and vehicle-carrying catamarans are to be encountered from one end of New Zealand to the other – from the Bay of Islands to the far north of the North Island and to Stewart Island off the most southerly point of the South Island. Two examples are now described.

Hauraki Gulf is a 4,000 sq. km area of water that lies between the city of Auckland and the Pacific Ocean. It is largely sheltered from the open ocean by the 80km-long Coromandel Peninsula and by the Great and Little Barrier Islands. Within the Gulf are numerous islands of which

Waiheke carries the largest population with 7,700 permanent inhabitants plus 3,400 second-homers.

The Gulf and its islands are served by an intensive network of ferries. Of these the largest operator is Fuller's Ferries, who operate a fleet of eight fast passenger vessels, mainly catamarans, between Auckland and Devonport (every quarter of an hour at peak and half-hourly off-peak); Northcoate Point, Birkenhead and Bayswater (some 20 return sailings daily); Waiheke Island (18 return sailings daily); Stanley Bay (11 return sailings); Halfmoon Bay (13 return sailings); and some of the smaller islands, harbour cruises, charters, etc.

About ten years ago I called unannounced at the Fullers HQ in Auckland seeking information about the company and its operations. The receptionist asked:

'Would you like to see any of the management?'

Readily assenting, I was taken upstairs to meet the chairman, George Hudson – a most delightful man of the old school who had worked his way up from humble beginnings. He noted my Norwegian surname and told me that he too was of Norwegian ancestry. The family had changed their name to Hudson during the First World War in response to the anti-foreigner prejudice then prevalent in New Zealand. He went on to describe the evolution of the company.

In 1981, he and his son, Douglas, saw the potential for a more modern ferry service and founded the Gulf Ferries Company, taking over the existing North Shore Ferries with its decrepit fleet. The transition from the slow, wooden vessels into a modern operation began in 1987 with the arrival of their first catamaran, the *Quickcat*. With a more comfortable and much faster vessel, the service to and from Waiheke Island was revolutionised. The fleet replacement continued and the company board was expanded. In 1988, the publicly listed Fullers Corporation Ltd went into receivership and its Auckland operation was bought by George and Keith who took on the Fullers brand to become the Fullers Group Limited. In 1998, Stagecoach New Zealand Limited became the major shareholder with George remaining as chairman.

More recently, in 2005, Infratil NZ bought all of Stagecoach's operations in Auckland, including Fullers. In 2007, after many successful years, George stepped down as chairman while Douglas became the CEO. In 2009 Fullers was sold to the Souter Holdings Group of companies, headed by Scotland's well known transport entrepreneur, Brian Souter.

Other ferry operators on the Hauraki Gulf include 360 Discovery, which offers a range of high-speed catamaran cruises on the Auckland Harbour to many of the smaller islands in the gulf and operates the only ferry service between Auckland and Coromandel. SeaLink operates a four-vessel vehicle ferry fleet on the shortest crossing to Waiheke Island from Half Moon Bay and Reuben's Water Taxis offers a flexible service to parts of the Gulf not served by other operators.

Stewart Island or Rakiura is New Zealand's third largest island, lying 19 miles (30km) south of the South Island across the Foveaux Straight. The permanent population is just over 400.

On the only opportunity I ever had to visit Stewart Island, the ferry from the South Island's most southerly port of Bluff was off because a Chinese freighter, the *Tai Ping*, with a cargo of fertiliser, had gone aground on the entrance to Bluff Harbour. She was due to be refloated on the noon high tide on my intended day of travel. Local wags had labelled the incident 'the *Tai Ping* error'. I had to drive back to Invercargill to catch one of the regular flights to the island.

A key purpose of the visit was to learn something of the ferry operation, and the following day I met up, as arranged, with Ian Munro, Managing Director of Stewart Island Marine Services at their office in the main settlement of Oban. He explained the background to the company's ferry business.

Until the late 1980s, Stewart Island was served by a heavily subsidised government-run mail ship *Wairua (II)* (1961–1985). She was a typical passenger cargo motorship of the period with derrick and hold forward and a crew of 15. The schedule was such that island travellers had to spend two nights on the mainland before they could return home. Then came a major shift in government policy.

Faced with a budget crisis, New Zealand's government decided to eliminate farm and other subsidies. This created a tough transition period for some farmers, but most proved to be skilled entrepreneurs, profitably restructuring their operations and exploring new markets. As part of the policy the Stewart Island mail ship subsidy was withdrawn and the service ceased.

Meanwhile Ian Munro, at that time a fisherman, and two other island businessmen had set up Stewart Island Marine Services and built a barge to service the island salmon farming industry. With the demise of the government mail ship, they arranged bank finance and had a 20-metre catamaran built in Fremantle. In 1991 the company commenced the passenger ferry service on the one-hour crossing to Bluff with the new 25-knot vessel providing two or more return trips daily, thereby revolutionising Stewart Island's connection with the outside world. Two further catamarans were built locally at Invercargill – the 20-metre *Southern Express* with a capacity for 62 passengers and the 23-metre *Foveaux Express* with a capacity for 97 passengers. Each vessel has a crew of 3, or 2 if fewer than 50 passengers are carried. Hydraulic cranes are fitted to handle general freight and parcels.

The Foveaux Straight can be rough but the catamarans cope well and are regarded as very good sea boats. The original catamaran was sold to the tour company Real Journeys who operate her as *Fiordland Flyer* on Lake Manapouri in connection with their Doubtful Sound cruises. In recent years Real Journeys have taken over the operation of the Stewart Island ferry which now trades as Stewart Island Experience.

There are few roads on Stewart Island and the demand for vehicle transportation is negligible. Vehicles, fuel and bulkier freight items are handled by a freight boat and other heavy loads are catered for by the dumb barge, utilised as required. The company employs 14 staff, of which half are land based. As with other New Zealand shipping operations, the ferry is unsubsidised, and yet is far superior to the former government-run service. Such has been its success, the population of Stewart Island, which had been in decline, is now growing again.

What is clear from these selected examples of ferry operations in other countries is that, while there is a common historical context, ferry developments in Norway, British Columbia and the Antipodes in their diverse ways have taken very different directions from Scottish practice over the last few decades. In Norway and British Columbia, the state has intervened to take radical steps to plan the route structure as part of the road network and to control fares. In Australia and New Zealand, highly innovative solutions have emerged although the public sector has little involvement other than in terms of maritime safety. In each case, however, cost-effective ferry operations have strengthened local economies and social mobility has improved.

Some common lessons emerge, however. These are:

- Frequency of service counts
- For a vehicle ferry, select the shortest feasible crossing to minimise cost and maximise frequency
- Select the most efficient vessel designs to minimise capital cost, crewing and fuel consumption
- Seek opportunities to utilise fast craft on passenger-only services to and from regional centres where potential traffic volumes can be generated

With these criteria in mind, it is now opportune to apply them to ascertain how Scottish ferries might be improved in a cost-effective manner.

CHAPTER 5

A BETTER FUTURE

SOME KEY PRINCIPLES

The Scottish Government seeks to enable us to 'live in sustainable places with access to amenities and services we need'. The challenge is to arrange ferry services to meet these aims.

Achieving community sustainability and a growing population implies developing confidence, on the one hand for business to invest in the local economy, and on the other hand for the local community to develop a quality of life that encourages people, and families in particular, to stay in their locale. Sustainability also implies reducing dependence on disproportionately high public funding and reducing environmental damage.

In the long run, reversing population decline will be a key indicator of success or failure. During the twentieth century most Scottish islands have suffered marked population decline. The population of the Western Isles, for example, is now about half its Edwardian level, indicating long-term economic decline relative to the rest of Scotland. Such decline is not inevitable. Other island communities such as the Isle of Man, the Faeroe Islands and, nearer to home, Skye, have shown marked increases in population and in prosperity.

Of course the fiscally autonomous administrations in the Isle of Man and the Faeroe Islands, notwithstanding very high ferry charges, have been able to focus on differentiating those economies to achieve economic growth in ways that are not open to the Western Isles. The Isle of Skye, however, has been able to sustain rapid economic and population growth over the last three decades within the same fiscal framework as that of the Western Isles. This is attributable, in part at least, to good transport links with the Scottish mainland partly due initially to a cheap and frequent ferry, then a toll bridge, from which the tolls were subsequently removed.

Depending on how they are provided, ferries can either be an impediment or an aid in achieving the Scottish Government's economic and social imperatives for sustainable communities.

To make progress, therefore, it is desirable to seek ferry connections geared to serve the economic and social advancement of our island and peninsular communities in as cost-effective and environmentally sustainable a manner as practicable. How this can be achieved will vary from case to case. In general terms, however, ferry schedules should, in broad order of priority, aim to make possible the following 'useful' journeys:

1. Daily access to and from the main Scottish centres without the need for an overnight stay en route
2. Day return access to a regional centre with adequate time for business or social purposes
3. Timings convenient to hauliers for the import of supplies and export of products
4. Timings useful to tourists to maximise visitor spend in the communities served
5. Daily commuting in either direction where distances are short
6. Evening travel to extend access opportunities in either direction for business and social travel

With these aims in mind we are set to envision a better future for our ferry services.

While the above aims are geared to improving access, the role of commercial cruise operators in contributing to the Scottish tourism economy has already been alluded to. Tourists pay for the experience of enjoying the county's heritage. Wealth and employment is created as a result. Incredible though it may seem, under current arrangements, passenger capacity and cost is regularly inflated on heavily subsidised ferry vessels to cater for round trip or non-landing cruise passengers. Thus instead of cruise passengers contributing to the economy, they are actually abstracting from it – the very reverse of sustainability.

From the experience of the more efficient operators in Scotland and in the wider world, a set of principles has emerged which can help focus policy to bring about the kinds of changes needed to improve how ferries are acquired and operated for the benefit of both local communities and the tax payer. These principles are:

- Shortest feasible crossings
- Efficient vessel design
- Cost-effective operation
- Competition and route tendering

SHORTEST FEASIBLE CROSSINGS

As has been demonstrated, short routes are self-evidently cheaper to operate, have shorter passage time, lower fares and charges, lower emissions, lower operating costs and subsidies (if any) and are more frequent. In this way they move towards road equivalence, reduce 'impedance' and stimulate traffic to the benefit of the economies and social well-being of the communities served – a multiple win. There are hundreds of such examples worldwide. In Scotland, to date, the concept seems, in the main, to have escaped the attention of those planning our ferry services, and the powerful traffic-generating effect of route shortening seems to have eluded the STAG process employed to examine transport investment options. This should be corrected.

There are actually quite a number of opportunities for route shortening in Scotland. They are:

- The Islay overland (via the Jura land-bridge)
- The Mull land-bridge to serve Coll, Tiree and Barra but alternated with direct Oban sailings
- Replace Oban–Lismore with Port Appin–Lismore
- Lochboisdale–Mallaig in place of Lochboisdale–Oban
- Splitting the Uig–Lochmaddy and Tarbert routes and in the long run substituting Dunvegan or Glendale (Loch Pooltiel) as the Lochmaddy landfall
- Gills Bay–Burwick in place of current Pentland Firth route
- Reorganise long Orkney and Shetland routes
- Fixed road links (i.e. causeways, bridges, tunnels etc.)

These proposals are examined in more detail below under the heading 'Route Alternatives'. Effective application, however, hinges on a number of technical and operational issues. The first hinges on the ferry vessels themselves.

EFFICIENT VESSEL PROCUREMENT

The very high potential cost of funding a replacement fleet has been signalled in the Ferry Plan. One option is the funding of new tonnage through private equity partnerships. The ostensible attraction is that it would remove the capital expenditure from the Scottish Government's capital programme. The downside, however, is that the long-term costs can be very high. The disproportionately high NorthLink subsidy is partly due to the private lease costs of the vessels coupled with their inefficient design and high operating cost. Private equity financing of the Isle of Man Steam Packet Company, which negotiated exclusive access to the Douglas ferry terminal with the government of the Isle of Man, has resulted in high ferry transport costs. Private equity funding coupled with exclusive rights, inefficient vessel design and high crew and fuel costs represents the very worst of all worlds in terms of long-term value for money and is to be avoided like the plague.

The selection of more economical and better-performing ships is a sounder approach. Encouraging private sector operators to source their own vessels – an attractive option when capital and operating costs per unit carried can be one third of those of a typical CMAL/ DMG vessel –has the potential to both reduce or even remove the capital expenditure on ferries from the Scottish Government's capital programme while encouraging operators to control operating costs so as to reduce operating subsidy. Such an approach would also create a pool of saleable vessels at times when tenders are up for renewal. Moving from large live-aboard crews to local shore-based crews working shifts reduces costs by removing the necessity for providing onboard accommodation and thereby sacrificing payload.

In a world context the range of vessel designs is huge but some examples offer particularly useful pointers. These are:

Medium-speed Vehicle-carrying Catamarans

Catamarans of this type have evolved in Australia to a high level of efficiency. Compared with conventional mono-hull ferries they have a low capital cost, high deadweight to displacement ratio (in other words, good payload), low consumption of clean fuel, low CO_2, good seakeeping, maneuverability and reliability, easy emergency evacuation characteristics and very economical operation. These vessels are available in a range of sizes to suit most operational requirements.

Pentland Ferries catamaran *Pentalina* is an example of this type that has proven herself on the demanding Pentland Firth crossing.

High Capacity RoPax Ferries
An INTERREG IIIB Northern Periphery Programme study compared the relative efficiency of the NorthLink ferries operating to Orkney and Shetland with other types of ferries on similar trades elsewhere. The study revealed that other vessels of similar capital cost, speed and passenger capacity were able to carry over four times the number of trailers compared with the NorthLink twins *Hjaltland* and *Hrossay*.

Clearly it is important to maximise carrying capacity and thereby increase revenue generation in proportion to operating cost. Improved lower-powered, high-capacity, multi-vehicle deck RoPax ferries may be suitable for cost-effective operation on some long distance routes:

High-speed Passenger Ferries
The Norwegians and Italians and more recently the Australians have pioneered high-speed passenger ferries. Nowadays large numbers are in service worldwide. They may be described as providing a high-quality coastal or island bus service. Typically these craft have a passenger capacity of up to 250, a crew of 3 or 4 and speeds of between 25 and 35 knots. The latest versions have smooth ride and low wash characteristics and capital cost of around £3 million. Because of their very low deadweight compared with a vehicle-carrying ferry, their fuel consumption is relatively low considering their high speed. These vessels can have a very useful niche role of providing a parallel fast passenger-only service to relieve a vehicle ferry service of peak foot passengers thereby allowing a reduction in crewing costs on the latter.

Medium-speed River Ferries
In Queensland, Australia, Brisbane CityCat provides a frequent fast river bus service with low wash 22-knot catamarans, a type of service that could be emulated on the River Clyde and/or possibly other sheltered water areas for relatively modest subsidy.

Other Vessel Options
Several independent operators have adopted cost-effective solutions to serve the needs of their market. These vary from comfortable saloon passenger craft such as those found on Loch Lomond, Loch

Ness and the Firths of Clyde and Forth; or simple but effective bow loaders with twin outboard propulsion as utilised at Kerrera; or the economical containership as operated by Streamline; or again rugged fast craft as used on the long and exposed run to St Kilda. The variety of such approaches underlines the importance of encouraging a range of independent operators in the interests of stimulating ingenuity and developing new wealth-creating business.

To illustrate how a more focussed approach could greatly reduce costs while bringing efficient new tonnage into service quickly, the Archipelago Philippine Ferry Corporation recently ordered ten catamarans of Stuart Ballantyne's design. The new 50m × 17m × 1.8m draft, quadruple-screw, 16-knot ships carry trucks, buses, cars and up to 500 passengers and cost around £7 million each; about a third that of conventional Scottish ferries of equivalent capacity. The fuel efficiency of these vessels is well ahead of the existing ferries, and standardised machinery, electronics and equipment ensure that the vessels and crew are totally interchangeable.

COST–EFFECTIVE OPERATION

The main cost components of ferry operation are capital (ships, terminals and roads), crew and fuel. The superiority of the private over the public sector as regards crewing and fuel consumption has been examined earlier. As with ships, a similar cost disparity is found in the development of terminals. Thus, if capital costs of ships, terminals, approach roads, etc. can be reduced, then lower financing costs (annualised to give comparison with running costs) will reduce the overall cost of a ferry operation.

Annualised Capital Costs Versus Running Costs

Ferries and non-trunk roads are funded separately such that replacement of a long route ferry by a short crossing, which may necessitate a new or upgraded road link, may place an unaffordable burden on a local authority.

This is one of the stumbling blocks in securing the benefits of shorter routes. With a few exceptions, such as Shetland Islands Council, there has, hitherto, been little co-ordination between road investment and ferry operations. This was well illustrated by the *Finlaggan* debacle on the Islay route already described.

Nowadays, local authorities cannot afford new road construction even where it is desirable to reduce costs and emissions and provide improved connections. To overcome this funding mismatch it will be necessary to create a means to offset savings to central government on ferry vessel (annualised) capital and running costs against cost to local authorities in providing link road and other capital improvements.

The Ferries Plan did not address this fundamental issue. It should have.

Air Services

Neither did the Ferries Plan mention air services and the complementary role they can play in aiding access to and from our island communities. In a number of cases, air services provide a viable supplement or alternative to ferries (e.g. Colonsay, Coll and Tiree, Orkney North Isles, etc.) and can offer a quality of connectivity that some ferry services cannot. Passenger air transport is also, in some cases, more cost-effective and less polluting than travel by large vehicle ferries. Ferry planning should take this into account and assess how the best balance between air and sea can be achieved.

A BETTER TENDERING SYSTEM

One of the most controversial aspects of the ferries consultation process has been the issue of tendering individual routes. The David Mac-Brayne Group, in the interest of self-preservation, has stated clearly that it did not favour route-by-route tendering and has successfully influenced stakeholders' opinion and the Scottish Government against such an eventuality.

Nevertheless, we have seen that where competitors to the DMG exist they have been able to attract new business through improved frequency while keeping operating costs well below those of the state operator. Had these competitors not existed, it would, perhaps, have been difficult to demonstrate that alternative operational models could both improve service levels and reduce costs. The fact that they do exist is surely proof enough that more widespread adoption of such techniques could yield very significant improvements in service quality and substantial savings in subsidy.

To that end the opening up of at least some individual routes to tender as originally suggested in the consultation document makes sense. If tenders on these routes are won by non-state operators, then a useful degree of pluralism will have been introduced to the Scottish ferry scene that will hopefully further illustrate the benefits of more cost-effective operation, so long as operators are given sufficient freedom to innovate. The tendering process should be simple, flexible and straightforward to give scope for bidders to come up with innovative solutions, for smaller operators have stated that the process is too complex and expensive. This is unfair to any business that does not have almost unlimited funds at its back.

Under a route-by-route tendering regime, it is likely that, given time to place orders, a number of operators would prefer to build their own tonnage. This is likely to encourage innovation and drive down costs. In that event CMAL would have a function in maintaining a reducing back-up fleet with the need for some replacement vessels but at a much lesser rate of investment than suggested in the Ferries Plan. Under no circumstance should operators be forced to lease costly CMAL vessels if they prefer to provide their own more efficient solutions. It may, however, be useful in the long term for CMAL to have one or two mothballed vessels in reserve to cover any future emergency.

Concern was expressed by Scottish Government officials that tendering individual routes would be more expensive administratively than dealing with one or two large bundles. While this may be so, the potential savings of tens of millions that could accrue from single-route tendering could greatly offset such a relatively small administrative element in the overall cost of ferry support. Creating a small team to handle route-by-route tenders on a rolling permanent basis would enable the process to be simplified and expertise to be built up.

It has also been argued by HITRANS and the DMG that route tendering would reduce the opportunity to provide cover in the event of breakdown. In practice, incoming operators would either provide at least two economical vessels to give the frequency necessary to develop their market, or would charter in tonnage at the time of the annual overhaul.

Tenders for single routes should be staggered over time although two or three routes may be issued for tender at one time. The tendering process should be ongoing year on year and need not be complex. To encourage innovation, the process should allow operators to come up with their own ideas and there should be built-in incentives to improve efficiencies. Local authorities undertake such tendering of bus and some ferry services on an ongoing and regular basis without undue difficulty.

Tenders should set out in brief the economic and social characteristics of the community to be served and ask how the tenderer proposes to advance these. This then provides the framework for proposed timings, frequency, capacity, fares, arrangements for onward travel, etc.

As climate change objectives are central to the Scottish Government's policies, these must be included within any future tendering exercise. Operators must be required to reduce their carbon footprint. The consultation document noted a conflict between improving journey times and reducing emissions, and that 'inevitably improved journey times require faster trips, which are likely to result in increased atmospheric emissions'. In practice this is by no means inevitable, as selection of shorter routes automatically reduces overall journey times, improves connections (i.e. frequency of service) and results in faster overall journeys, reduced emissions and unit costs.

Emissions objectives should be defined on a 'per unit conveyed' basis such that traffic growth reflecting economic and population growth is not penalised. Inclusion of appropriate climate change considerations would incentivise tendering parties to look to low-carbon solutions including less-polluting fuels such as LNG and, in the long run, hydrogen.

ROUTE ALTERNATIVES

As a general rule, the more vehicle traffic generated by ferry, the more economic and social development will be stimulated. Alternative ferry route options described below will demonstrate how shorter crossings and efficient vessel design can achieve a much more cost-effective and environmentally friendly operation as compared with the current pattern of service.

2010 traffic figures for each route are listed in Appendix 1 and vessel-carrying capacities and power are listed in Appendix 2.

Arran

The 11.5 nautical miles crossing between Ardrossan and Brodick (Arran, pop. 5,000) is provided year round by the large 15-knot *Caledonian Isles*. The passage time is 55 minutes and most days five return crossings are provided, the last mainland departure being 6 p.m., except Fridays when an 8.30 p.m. sailing is provided. From 2007 the former Rothesay ferry *Saturn* provided a high season supplementary service. Commuting to the mainland is frustrated, however, by the infrequent ferry passage, the 8.20 morning departure from Brodick being too late to arrive on the mainland for normal start of work time, coupled with the very early evening cessation of the service.

To overcome these handicaps a radical change in the style of operation would revolutionise Arran's mainland access. Employment in summer of two medium-speed catamarans with a service speed of 17 knots and a capacity for, say, 400 passengers and 80 cars could, in theory, provide an hourly service. In winter a service every two hours with one vessel running into the late evening would be adequate. The turnaround time is admittedly tight.

Based on the experience of Pentland Ferries the capital cost of cata-marans of the type suggested would be around £10–12 million apiece, compared with the replacement cost of *Caledonian Isles*, estimated to be in the region of £30 million. Initial calculation suggests that the traffic-generating potential of such a service could be substantial and reflected over time in economic and population growth on Arran. Such a service would enable two-way daily commuting which is not possible at present. The key to making an operation of this kind cost effective would be the employment of shore-based crews working in shifts with the main year-round vessel being based in Arran, thereby boosting employment on the island.

Ardrossan is difficult for vessels to enter in certain weather conditions. Highly manoeuvrable catamarans are more likely to overcome these difficulties than the current large class of vessel.

The 'back-door' 5.2 nautical miles crossing between Lochranza, Arran and Claonaig, Kintyre is served by a Loch-class vessel provid-ing 8 or 9 return sailings daily in summer with a 30-minute passage time. As *Caledonian Isles* has a fully enclosed vehicle deck, she is not permitted to carry hazardous cargoes. Petrol tankers must, therefore, use the Lochranza route to supply Arran with motor spirit. A restricted winter service is provided between Tarbert, Loch Fyne and Lochranza mainly as a hazardous cargo link. Extending the schedule to year-round operation would require some increase in subsidy but as the operating costs of this type of vessel are relatively modest, it is assumed that this could be made up from savings on other routes.

Cowal

The background to the competition between Western Ferries and the former CalMac/Cowal Ferries Dunoon–Gourock antiquated side-loading service has been described in Chapter 2. As, latterly, Western Ferries profitably carried almost 90 per cent of vehicular traffic between Cowal and Inverclyde, there has been no practical justification for continuing to carry a handful of vehicles at a loss on the longer passage between Dunoon and Gourock. There was, however, some sense in maintaining a direct passenger connection with the Gourock rail head and, as of 2011, Argyll Ferries, a subsidiary of the DMG, commenced a subsidised passenger-only service on the route, leaving Western Ferries to concentrate on vehicular traffic, which as of 2012 amounts to some 600,000 vehicles annually.

The new passenger service operates with two vessels, *Argyll Flier* and the somewhat inadequate *Ali Cat*, on a half-hourly schedule running from early till late. The schedule is a big improvement on the former Gourock–Dunoon vehicle ferry. There has, however, been concern about cancellations of sailings in adverse weather. Virtually all ferry services suffer some weather disruption but Dunoon is fortunate in having Western Ferries' very frequent and reliable vehicle ferry service, with good bus connections as an alternative. Some years ago a new RO-RO terminal was constructed at Dunoon to enable vehicle ferry end loading. This has never been used for that purpose, but is now used rather awkwardly for embarking and landing passengers over the stern of the passenger vessels. The normal arrangement for berthing small passenger ferries would be side loading by means of a pontoon, for which the north face of Dunoon old pier would be suitable.

There is a small but vociferous lobby in Dunoon pledged to maintain a town-centre-to-town-centre vehicle ferry between Dunoon and Gourock despite the fact that it is uneconomic, environmentally damaging and, contrary to EU state aids rules, would require subsidy. In fact transport policy is normally concerned to *remove* vehicular traffic from town centres, not encourage it.

It was with some surprise that in July 2013 the £50,000 Gourock Dunoon Ferry Feasibility Study purported to demonstrate that a ferry service can be created between the two ports whereby the carriage of passengers is subsidised, but the carriage of vehicles is not. I can't remember when, if ever, I witnessed such an expensive, contorted and blatantly biased attempt to justify the unjustifiable. The study's assumed costs and revenue growth projections seem highly questionable and the assumed comparative specifications for passenger-only and vehicle ferries are wholly unreasonable. The study did not even consider the adverse effect on Western Ferries of the introduction of a subsidised parallel vehicle ferry.

A key cause of the relative unreliability of the current passenger service, in so far as it is required at all, is the selection of two small vessels for half-hourly operation rather than a single more robust passenger vessel operating on an hourly schedule. This would be more than adequate for the traffic on offer and still far in excess of the ferry provision enjoyed by most other communities. This option was not even considered in the study. Neither were the greatly increased CO_2 emissions attributable to the proposed options taken into account. All of this must surely render the whole proposition unfeasible.

Bearing in mind the appalling track record of our state-subsidised ferry planners in grossly underestimating the costs of new ferry proposals, it is to be hoped that our politicians will not be taken in by this latest fantasy.

Bute

Ferry services to Bute (pop. 7,228) have some peculiar characteristics. The connection with the Wemyss Bay railhead is operated by two identical 60-car drive-through vessels, *Argyll* and *Bute*. Oddly while the train service is hourly, the ships run every three-quarters of an hour, thereby making a train connection only on alternate sailings. As with other CalMac routes, sailings cease in the early evening, so reducing the opportunity for social and business travel. The Ferry Plan offered little advice as to how this anomaly might be addressed other than alluding to the expense of running later, this being a function of the large crew (compared with, say, Western Ferries).

Bute's frequent back-door ferry route across the Kyles of Bute between slipways at Colintraive (Cowal) and Rhubodach (Bute), a crossing of about 400 metres, is operated by the 36-car, 4-crew, double-ended *Loch Dunvegan*. This vessel is rather larger and more expensive to operate than necessary for such a short crossing. The Ferry Plan sensibly suggested extending the operating hours until late evening. Astonishingly this was opposed by Argyll and Bute Council. As far back as the 1960s the then local authorities were looking at the feasibility of a bridge across this relatively short water gap. In the half century since then, nothing has come of this proposal. One wonders why.

Islay and Jura

The current Islay (pop. 3,457) service operates between Kennacraig (Kintyre) and alternative Islay ports of Port Askaig and Port Ellen, each crossing being 26 and 30 nautical miles respectively. The timetable varies somewhat from day to day. On most days three return sailings are provided between Kennacraig and Port Ellen, and there is one Port Askaig return trip. On Wednesdays two calls are made at Port Askaig, one being extended to Colonsay and Oban.

The route is normally operated by two ships: the older *Hebridean Isles*, and the new £24.5 million *Finlaggan* with a highly polluting power output of 8,000kW. The new vessel necessitated the £12.8 million expansion of the ferry terminal at Port Askaig, which has pushed the alignment further into the fierce Sound of Islay tide races, making berthing more difficult. A further £5 million of expenditure was required at Port Ellen and £9 million at Kennacraig to enable *Finlaggan* to berth – a total project cost so far of £51.3 million. This huge sum does not take account of the cost of replacing *Hebridean Isles* at an estimated £25 million. Over and above this total capital requirement of some £76 million, there is an ongoing annual subsidy requirement estimated at some £8 million.

Jura (pop. 188) has no direct mainland connection other than the seasonal daily passenger RIB to Tayvallich. The short, frequent ferry between Feolin and Port Askaig, Islay, which makes connection with the relatively infrequent calls there by CalMac, is otherwise the only scheduled link with the outside world.

As a more effective alternative to the current pattern of service, as mooted by the Highland Transport Board of 1967, and indeed before that, there has been pressure for the creation of an overland route that would give quicker and very much more frequent access to Islay and Jura. The scheme would upgrade the current Feolin crossing and introduce a second ferry service between Lagg (Jura) and Keills or Loch Sween (Knapdale). The assumed high cost of upgrading the road through Jura and from Crinan to Keills has been stated as the main reason why the scheme has not been progressed. Sections of the Jura, Keills and Tayvallich populations are also opposed to the scheme on grounds of increased traffic.

A dedicated vehicle ferry between Jura and the Scottish mainland over the shortest feasible crossing would reinstate the traditional droving route. The crossing at that point is around five nautical miles and for a vessel such as an 11-knot, 35-car, 150-passenger Sea Transport Corporation catamaran, the passage time would be some 30 minutes to Keills or 40 minutes to a suitable sheltered landing near Dunrosta on the east shore of Loch Sween. At the Jura side, recent forestry extraction by sea has utilised a temporary floating pier and such could be employed in the first instance for a vehicle ferry. A single vessel could maintain a two-hourly frequency from, say, 7 a.m. till after 10 p.m.

The vessel would berth overnight in Jura, the more sheltered harbour, and the ten crew jobs (two and a half crews) would be Jura-based. The vessel would have a power output of 700kW (less than a tenth that of *Finlaggan*, with a proportionate reduction in CO_2 emissions) and cost some £4 million (one sixth the cost of *Finlaggan*). A short, frequent crossing of the type outlined above, however, would represent a step change in the accessibility of Jura and Islay such that it would be possible to drive to Glasgow or Edinburgh for a day's business and return home the same evening.

A comparison of overall journey times between Port Ellen and Lochgilphead is shown below:

Overland	Miles	Time Mins	CO_2/car
Port Ellen–Port Askaig	21	35	1.65
Terminal wait time		15	
Ferry Passage		10	5.00
Feolin–Lagg	17.5	25	1.37
Terminal wait time		15	
Ferry Passage		30	11.00
Keills–Lochgilphead	18	30	1.41
Total		160	20.44
Via Kennacraig			
Terminal wait time		30	
Port Ellen–Kennacraig		120	150.00
Kennacraig–Lochgilphead	19	27	2.12
Total		177	152.12

Thus from Port Ellen the overland is 17 minutes quicker; from Port Askaig, almost an hour quicker. In addition the much greater frequency gives many more useful journey options. It will also be noted that a car (and its proportion of ferry emissions) taken over the overland will emit about one seventh the CO_2 compared with the Kennacraig route.

Total replacement of the Kennacraig route will of course necessitate major road improvements in Jura and Knapdale. To get an idea of cost, the recently completed high-specification Broadford to Armadale road in Skye through similar terrain as on Jura and Knapadale cost just over £1 million per mile. On that basis, the cost of upgrading the 35 or some miles (56km) between Feolin and Lochgilphead may be estimated at some £40 million. Two new ferries at £4 million each and terminal works of £2 million, gives a grand total of around £50 million, well below the £76 million capital commitment for the current system.

A key issue has always been the burden such a capital expenditure would place on the local authority. To resolve this the cost of such 'ferry link' road works should, as suggested by the Highland Transport Board, be borne by central government, i.e. nowadays Transport Scotland. The big saving, however, is in operating costs and therefore subsidy. It has been estimated that the subsidy saving to Transport Scotland would be at least £5 million per year, (even taking account of ongoing road maintenance costs) or £100 million over 20 years.

While the benefits of the overland scheme are obvious enough, its full implementation would represent a radical shift in policy. As a short-term, halfway house, the locally based Overland Route Company Ltd have proposed introducing a small vehicle ferry between Lagg and Loch Sween to give Jura a direct mainland link for cars and light vehicles. Under this option freight traffic and most Islay traffic would continue to be routed via Kennacraig.

Colonsay

Colonsay (pop. 108) has in many respects been Scotland's most isolated populated island. The winter service of three round trips weekly from Oban on the 32 nautical miles passage takes 2 hours 20 minutes. The run is normally provided either by *Lord of the Isles* or *Isle of Mull*. In winter these large vessels, capable of carrying many times the entire population of the island, run virtually empty and there are few occasions when the number of passengers outnumbers the crew. In summer the service is increased to five Oban round trips. There is a weekly connection to and from Port Askaig, Islay: a 14-nautical mile passage taking 1 hour 10 minutes. Although summer traffic is augmented by cruise passengers, year-round landings on Colonsay are light. The schedule is such that, until recently, secondary school children who must board in Oban could not get home at weekends throughout the term, nor could islanders go to the mainland without spending at least one night away from home.

To relieve these issues, in my last year with Highlands and Islands Enterprise, I initiated research into the feasibility of an air service between Oban, Colonsay and other outlying Argyll islands. It took a few years of negotiation, but it gave me much pleasure to see the service become operational to provide hitherto unavailable day-return travel and, most importantly, to allow schoolkids home for the weekend.

As regards a better future for Colonsay's ferry connections, the Ferry Plan recommends transfer of the current Small Isles vessel *Lochnevis* to become Colonsay's dedicated vessel. Although larger and more expensive to operate than is required for the population served, this proposal should permit much improved scheduling, although timetable proposals have not been announced. Ideally, the best solution would be to base a vehicle ferry of appropriate size, with a crew of, say, 3 or 4 and passenger certificate for, say, 70, at Colonsay. Crewed by local personnel, the service could be geared to suit local needs, running to both Oban and Port Askaig as required. This would, however, require the creation of a sheltered harbour. If the Jura overland route is developed and a spur road built to West Loch Tarbert, Jura, it would be possible to introduce a short, frequent 14-nautical mile crossing to Colonsay with a dedicated vessel and onward frequent overland connection with the mainland. Such an option, if feasible, is well in the future.

Mull

The Oban–Craignure (Mull, pop. 2,667) route has much in common with Ardrossan–Arran. The 9.5-nautical miles crossing is provided by the large 15-knot *Isle of Mull*. The passage time is 45 minutes. In summer five to seven return crossings are provided daily. In winter this reduces to between three and five crossings with the last departure from Oban being 4 p.m., except Friday and Saturday when a later sailing is scheduled. This schedule prevents the development of commuting between Mull and Oban.

As with Arran, two medium-speed catamarans of, say, 400 passengers summer capacity, each providing an hourly service in summer and with one vessel every two hours in winter running into the late evening year round, would revolutionise Mull's connectivity.

Mull attracts a considerable seasonal foot passenger day-trip clientele. To supplement the summer peaks and provide additional fast commuter connections between Oban, Craignure, Lochaline and Tobermory, as well as summer cruises, a high-speed passenger vessel (with three crew) may be an economic option that would help open up the Oban–Sound of Mull area for commuting and new settlement.

The short, frequent Lochaline–Fishnish service is a useful, economical and environmentally acceptable 'back door' to and from Mull with handy road connections to the north and east. It carries around 25 per cent of vehicles leaving or entering Mull. The main drawback is the very restricted hours of operation, the last sailing to Mull normally being 16.45, which prevents any opportunity to develop two-way commuting or evening social travel. As the operating cost of this service is at a very much lower level than the Craignure route (see Appendix 3), extending the hours of operation to 22.00 or later through shift working would be enormously beneficial in generating traffic to the enhancement of the economies on both sides of the sound and need not incur prohibitive costs.

A second Mull 'back door', the Kilchoan–Tobermory 35-minute crossing, provides seven return trips daily in summer and three in winter. Annual carryings are light at about 3 per cent of the total vehicles entering and leaving Mull. It nevertheless provides access to the services of Tobermory for the population of the Ardnamurchan Peninsula. The operating hours are woefully restricted and seem almost designed to discourage development of regular contact between the communities. The winter schedule does not permit commuting from Ardnamurchan to Tobermory, as the last sailing from the Mull port is 15.45 (18.00 in summer). To aid the development of Tobermory as a regional centre, to encourage settlement and economic development and to grow traffic and revenue, a more useful commuter schedule should be developed with longer operating hours.

Lismore

The services to Lismore (pop. 147) are the wrong way round, with a passenger-only ferry on the very short ten-minute crossing to Port

Appin and an infrequent vehicle ferry on the long 50-minute Oban route. Substituting a frequent vehicle ferry at Port Appin, as suggested in the Ferry Plan, would have the effect of providing vehicular access at a greatly reduced cost to the user and a concomitant reduction in subsidy and CO_2 emissions. In fact the drive to Oban is quicker than the long sea journey. If a high-speed passenger commuter vessel were employed on the Oban–Sound of Mull station, it may be possible to include Lismore in its roster at minimal cost.

Coll and Tiree

The ferry service between Coll (pop. 164), Tiree (pop. 770) and Oban is part of a complex roster of vessels also serving Barra, Lochboisdale, Colonsay, etc. The two vessels mainly concerned are *Lord of the Isles* and *Clansman*. The winter schedule for the long (52 nautical miles) passage offers four round trips per week with an early morning departure, usually 06.45. The round trip takes eight and a quarter hours. A daily service is provided in summer. If island residents need to travel for business or social purposes to the mainland they have to spend at least one night away from home in summer and two nights in winter. In view of the journey length and infrequency of the service, traffic is light.

The solution to reducing the isolation of these islands lies partially in an overland operation, using Mull as a land-bridge. A HITRANS study purported to demonstrate that this option was unviable on environmental and journey time grounds. This conclusion was shown to have been based on wholly flawed assumptions and that in fact the land-bridge, if used in conjunction with direct daily Oban sailings and a more economical vessel could much improve journey time and environmental performance while doubling frequency with a hitherto unavailable range of useful connections. See the suggested timetable below.

This schedule would give two return sailings daily, offering useful midday departure, and a mid-afternoon arrival at Oban, thereby permitting same-day access to and from the Central Belt and beyond every day, an option that is not available at present.

There is a need to upgrade the section of road between Tobermory and Salen, with Tobermory as the land-bridge landfall for Coll and Tiree.

Oban	dep.	07.00	z
Tobermory	dep.	..	13.40
Coll	arr.	09.40	15.10
Tiree	arr.	10.45	16.00
Tiree	dep.	11.00	16.15
Coll	dep.	12.00	17.15
Tobermory	arr.	13.20	..
Oban	arr.	x	20.00

x = connection arrives Oban approx. 1 hr 30 min. later
z = connection departs Oban approx. 1 hr 30 min. earlier
.. = Assumes no stop at Tobermory. A stop could be made if desired.

The shortest crossing between Mull and Coll at nine nautical miles is to and from Calgary on the far west of Mull. In fact nearby Port na Bà ('cattle port' in Gaelic) at Croig was the landing place for cattle and mails from Coll in the days before powered navigation. From that area a relatively frequent service could be created, subject to improvement of the Calgary road. If a fixed link were created between Coll and Tiree, a two-hourly rotation could be provided from early morning till late evening giving up to nine sailings per day in each direction – a massive step change in improving access to and from these islands. This may be regarded as a long-term ambition.

Barra and South Uist

Castlebay, Barra (pop. 1,172 with Vatersay) and Lochboisdale, South Uist (pop. 1,818) are currently served from Oban by Lord of the Isles and Clansman as described previously. The passage distance is 78 nautical miles between Oban and either port. The winter schedule offers a four times a week sailing for Oban–Barra–Lochboisdale. The passage time for Oban–Barra is around five hours, and six and a half hours to Lochboisdale via Barra. An additional round trip sailing is given on Fridays. The summer schedule is effectively daily at varying timings, mostly with separate direct sailings to Barra and Lochboisdale. The route is expensive to operate, but long passage distance, low frequency and inconvenient timings mean traffic is light. In terms of passengers, the service is running at only around 15 per cent of capacity on average, which begs the question as to why vessels with such large passenger certificates and crews are utilised on the service. The average capacity utilisation by vehicles is around 25 per cent.

It is worth bearing in mind that the combined steaming of the Coll/ Tiree and Barra/Lochboisdale sailings up and down the sound of Mull consumes some 20,000 tonnes of fuel annually, bringing with it a substantial environmental price in terms of emissions as well as a heavy economic cost. As with Coll and Tiree, a landfall at Tobermory instead of Oban on certain days would obviate much of this. See suggested timetable below.

		MWF	TThSSu	MWF
Castlebay	*dep.*	07.00	08.00	15.00
Tobermory	*arr.*	10.15	..	18.15
Oban	*arr.*	x	13.00	x
Oban	*dep.*	z	15.00	z
Tobermory	*dep.*	10.45	..	18.45
Castlebay	*arr.*	14.00	20.00	22.00

x = Connection arrives Oban approx. 1 hr 30 min. later
z = Connection departs Oban approx. 1 hr 30 min. earlier
.. = Assumes no stop at Tobermory. A stop could be made if desired.

This timetable would enable two return sailings daily on the days that Tobermory was used and permit a full afternoon's business in Oban. A South Uist connection would be possible via the Eriskay–Barra ferry.

As regards South Uist there has been an ambition for a shorter and more frequent link with Mallaig, a passage of 47 nautical miles. An illustrative timetable is set out below.

Lochboisdale	*dep.*	07.00	15.00
Mallaig	*arr.*	10.15	18.15
Mallaig	*dep.*	10.45	18.45
Lochboisdale	*arr.*	14.00	22.00

Such a service would allow a full afternoon's business by islanders in Fort William – an unprecedented level of mainland access for Uist. A daily connection between Barra and Mallaig via the Barra–Eriskay ferry would also be possible.

It has recently been stated by 'official sources' that a new £24 million vessel would be required for a Lochboisdale–Mallaig service – in other words, a replica *Finlaggan*. How absurd. With a doubling of frequency, a vessel of significantly less passenger capacity (say 250 maximum) and power (say 4,000kW maximum) and crew (say 12 shore-based maximum), would comfortably deal with the increased demand created by the new service. If based on *Pentalina*, the cost for appropriate Barra, South Uist and Coll/Tiree vessels would be between £7 million and £9 million apiece.

The Small Isles

The ferry service between Mallaig and the Small Isles of Eigg (pop. 67), Muck (pop. 30), Rum (pop. 22) and Canna (pop. 12) is provided by the purpose-built 13-knot ferry *Loch Nevis*. While all islands are equipped with slipways to load and discharge vehicles, vehicles may only be landed by special permission and numbers carried are, therefore, very limited. The underlying schedule is in the form of a daily round trip to the islands from Mallaig allowing time ashore on some islands on certain days. It is not normally possible for islanders to visit the mainland and return the same day. The subsidy level is phenomenal at some £250 per passenger carried and some £26,000 per island inhabitant. Incredible though it may seem, a significant proportion of passengers are non-landing round-trip cruise passengers who cost much and contribute nothing to the island economies.

A summer passenger service is provided daily by private operator Arisaig Marine on the shorter route between Arisaig and Eigg, the most populous island, with extended trips to Rum or Muck on alternate days. This unsubsidised service lands as many passengers on these islands as the hugely subsidised state operation.

As Arisaig is the nearest landfall to Eigg (7.5 nautical miles as compared with 10.5 to Mallaig), it would be possible to provide a more frequent ferry service between Arisaig and Eigg and Muck with a more economical vessel. This would allow a range of journeys, including mainland day visits, that are not currently possible, all at reduced subsidy. Carriage of vehicles could be arranged by charter of *Spanish John*. New Zealand's Stewart Island ferry service across the Foveaux Strait to and from Bluff offers an interesting model.

Armadale (Skye)

The current summer service of eight daily return crossings over this 30-minute, 4.4-nautical mile passage across the Sound of Sleat is provided in by the double-ended 14-knot *Coruisk*. In winter a restricted service of only two return sailings is provided by the Small Isles vessel.

A key deficiency of this service, as with others described, is that it is not possible to use the ferry to commute between Sleat, Skye and Mallaig. To overcome the lack of a commuter service, the timetable should be recast to permit arrival at Mallaig before 09.00 on a year-round basis plus extended operating hours into the evening.

Raasay

The vehicle ferry service between Sconser (Skye) and the new terminal near Raasay House (Raasay, pop. 192) is the test bed for the new hybrid diesel–electric ferry *Hallaig*. This double-ended 22-car capacity vessel has been promoted as a 'low emission' solution, using, as it does, an electrical plug-in to supplement the diesel power unit. A 20 per cent saving in emissions has been claimed. The £11 million build price, however, is two and a half times that of a conventional ferry of greater capacity, yet analysis by Professor Alf Baird of Napier University has demonstrated that, compared with more efficient diesel mechanical vessels, there are no savings in emissions per vehicle or passenger.

North Uist and Harris

The shortest links currently between the Western Isles and the mainland are those between Uig (Skye) and, alternately, Lochmaddy (North Uist) and Tarbert (Harris) at 26 and 25.4 nautical miles respectively. These are not, however, the shortest feasible links, which are Loch Pooltiel (Glendale, Skye)–Lochmaddy and Kilmaluag (North Trotternish, Skye)–Scalpay, each about 16 nautical miles.

One of the most unsatisfactory features of the two Uig routes is that they are operated by the same large vessel, the 16.5-knot *Hebrides*. In summer this ship provides two departures from Lochmaddy on Mondays, Wednesdays, Fridays, Saturdays and Sundays and but one departure at a different time on the intervening days. On alternate days Tarbert receives the two and one pattern. The daily variation in times has been described as 'a knitting pattern' – incomprehensible to most people. The inconvenient timetabling and low frequency could be satisfactorily resolved by providing two vessels – one dedicated to each route. Such a solution may seem to have the effect of increasing rather than reducing costs, but coupled with route shortening and using more economical vessels, this effect can be more than mitigated. To illustrate this, a modern vessel of appropriate size dedicated to the

Lochmaddy–Glendale crossing could undertake five or six return trips within an eighteen-hour day.

On such a frequency, a shore-based crew of around 12, a passenger capacity of 250 and a car capacity 80 could provide well over twice the current route capacity of *Hebrides*. To illustrate the radical improvement a service pattern of this kind would bring a suggested schedule is set out below.

Lochmaddy	*dep.*	06.00	09.00	12.00	15.00	18.00	21.00
Glendale (Loch Pooltiel)	*arr.*	07.10	10.10	13.10	16.10	19.10	22.10
Glendale (Loch Pooltiel)	*dep.*	07.30	10.30	13.30	16.30	19.30	22.30
Lochmaddy	*arr.*	08.40	11.40	14.40	17.40	20.40	00.10

Such near-road equivalence would for the first time create a short sea bridge to the Western Isles with very significant potential for driving forward economic regeneration. Although the overall operating costs could increase somewhat, it has been calculated that traffic would triple due to much-improved frequencies and regularity. This increase in traffic would more than offset increased operating costs, substantially reducing the need for subsidy. Lest it be thought that such an increase is unrealistic, it still represents a level of traffic well below that enjoyed by the Isle of Mull, which has a similar number of inhabitants as the Uists.

The Glendale option would, however, require a road upgrade of the B884 between Lonmore and Loch Pooltiel which, coupled with the need to build a new terminal on the site of the old steamer pier at Loch Pooltiel, would cost an estimated £20 million. This investment annualised at £1.5 million would be offset by the substantially increased revenues generated by the improved service. In the shorter term, however, and pending such an investment, utilising Dunvegan as the Skye landfall could present a compromise solution.

As mentioned, the shortest crossing between Skye and Harris is between the northernmost point of Skye's Trotternish peninsula at Kilmaluag. There is in fact a place nearby called Rubha na h-Aiseig ('ferry headland' in Gaelic), a reminder, it seems, of droving times when cattle from Harris were shipped by the shortest crossing to the nearest landfall in Skye. The development of such a short crossing may be regarded as a long-term possibility, offering a similar schedule to that illustrated above for Lochmaddy. Meantime a significant improvement in service would result from the substitution of an economical vessel dedicated to the existing Uig and Tarbert route, thereby more than doubling the frequency to up to four return trips per day as demonstrated below.

Tarbert	*dep.*	07.00	11.00	15.00	19.00
Uig	*arr.*	08.40	12.40	16.40	20.40
Uig	*dep.*	09.00	13.00	17.00	21.00
Tarbert	*arr.*	10.40	14.40	18.40	22.40

A two-ship service along the lines described above would revolutionise access to and from the Western Isles, for the first time making possible almost all the complete range of useful journeys set out at the beginning of this chapter.

Lewis

The Stornoway–Ullapool passenger and vehicle ferry route has been operated by the 18-knot *Isle of Lewis*, the basic pattern of service on the 45.5 nautical mile, 2 hour 45 minute passage being 2 return sailings daily, augmented on peak summer Wednesdays and Fridays by an additional return sailing. On this route the pattern of sailings is such that normally departure and arrival times are standard from day to day. The Stornoway service has been augmented by a chartered freight vessel *Muirneag* which makes a return trip overnight between Stornoway and Ullapool while *Isle of Lewis* is inactive.

In 2012 the decision was taken to replace both vessels with one vessel, larger than any so far in the CMAL/CalMac fleet. The 116-metre, 22-knot *Loch Seaforth*, currently being built for the extraordinary cost of £43 million, will be capable of operating 24 hours a day with a capacity for up to 700 passengers, and 143 cars or 20 commercial vehicles, a carrying capacity not significantly greater than the combined capacity of the current *Isle of Lewis* and *Muirneag*. The new vessel is scheduled for delivery in June 2014.

Operating one large ship on the route is an expensive and retrograde mistake with serious multiple disadvantages. Furthermore, accommodating the large crew takes up valuable passenger space, while disgorging large pulses of traffic on to the Ullapool–Inverness road will intensify frustration and compromise road safety. The despoiling of the

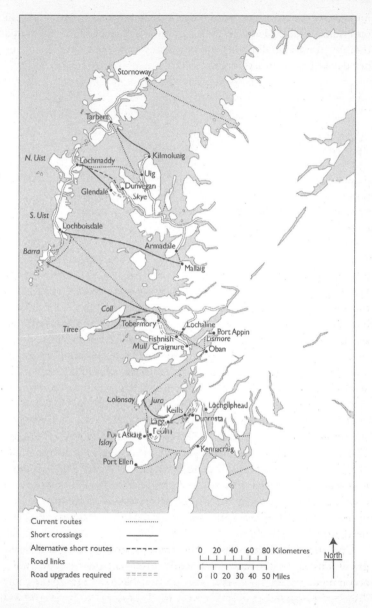

Short Crossing Opportunities

Ullapool waterfront for the expanded car park/marshalling area also impacts adversely on the village's attractiveness upon which its tourist trade depends.

Discussion with a Scottish-based commercial consortium indicated that a pair of 85-metre vessels of modern design, of proven seakeeping and fuel economy characteristics would collectively have greater capacity than the planned new single large vessel and could be operated for approximately half the cost, resulting in a very substantial reduction in subsidy requirement. Furthermore, the increased frequency of service would of itself generate new traffic, thereby enhancing the Lewis economy and further reducing the subsidy requirement.

One further option is the relocation of the mainland terminal to Aultbea, which would reduce steaming time by about half an hour with concomitant reduction of operating costs.

Caithness–Orkney

Services across the Pentland Firth have been described in earlier chapters. The NorthLink Stromness–Scrabster service requires a subsidy of circa £10 million. In contrast, Pentland Ferries' high-quality, fast, frequent, self-funding ferry connection on the shorter Gills Bay–St Margaret's Hope crossing now carries the majority of cars across the Firth, and effectively renders the NorthLink Stromness–Scrabster service obsolete. Closure of the longer NorthLink route would save between £6 and £10 million per year and eliminate its heavy emissions, even compared with an enhanced two-vessel, more frequent service on the shorter route.

Using a small part of the savings to upgrade Burwick terminal, the nearest Orkney landfall at nine nautical miles would reduce the passage distance further and enable an hourly service in summer and two hourly in winter. Channelling all Pentland Firth vehicular traffic over Burwick would increase traffic to an estimated 400,000 passengers, 140,000 cars and 16,000 commercial vehicles. The benefit of such greatly improved access to Orkney's economy and social well-being would be substantial. Lest these figures should seem overoptimistic, this computed car traffic level is less than one fifth of that carried by Western Ferries.

Orkney and Shetland Long Haul

The phenomenal subsidy and massive CO_2 emissions on the long-haul overnight vehicle ferry service operated between Aberdeen and Kirkwall (Orkney) and Lerwick (Shetland) has already been described in some detail. The route is operated by two 24-knot sister ships *Hjaltland* and *Hrossey*. Clearly the very high NorthLink subsidy is accounted for by the unsuitability of the vessels for the trade. Because of their limited capacity for trailers, the operation is supplemented by two freighters, *Hildasay* and *Helliar*.

Shetland sailings are alternatively direct or via Kirkwall (Orkney). Since 2010, the freight traffic between Aberdeen and Kirkwall has increased at the expense of the Pentland Firth due to an increase in subsidised freighter frequency. Passenger and car numbers between Aberdeen and Orkney are, however, a tiny fraction of those using either the Pentland Firth or the air links. In view of the high financial and environmental cost of the service between north-east Scotland and Orkney/Shetland, a complete rethink is required. As it is both much cheaper and significantly less environmentally damaging to send passengers, cars and freight overland to the north of Scotland than by ferry, it is highly questionable if there is a need for an Aberdeen–Orkney passenger vehicle ferry service at all.

For Shetland what is suggested is replacement of the current NorthLink fleet with two much more economical, say 14-knot, RoPax vessels, configured mainly for freight but with some passenger capacity for year-round nightly operation. Because of the restriction on the size of vessels that can use Aberdeen, that port would be unavailable for a high-capacity RoPax vessel. There would be advantage, therefore, in selecting Peterhead as the landfall port, the further advantage being that it is available in all weather conditions (Aberdeen is not) and would save two hours steaming/berthing and, therefore, fuel and emissions. Isles travellers would actually be in Aberdeen city centre and station quicker by car or coach connection than if the ship sailed direct.

To augment summer capacity, a seasonal daily return service between Sumburgh, Shetland and Gills Bay, Caithness configured mainly for passengers and cars could for the first time give Shetlanders the opportunity to travel to and from any part of Scotland by sea and land with their car, or by coach connection in daylight. Such a link would also provide a daily link between Orkney and Shetland via Caithness.

Orkney South and North Isles

Orkney Ferries run the current vehicle ferry service between Longhope and Lyness on the island of Hoy (pop. 360), Flotta (pop. 81) and Houton on the Orkney Mainland, together with the Stromness–Graemsay–Moness service. There is also a private fast catamaran passenger service between Houton and the Talisman oil terminal on Flotta.

Although much delayed, Lyness has been proposed as a site for a major container transshipment terminal whose development is a stated priority for the Scottish Government. If and when this important development comes on stream, demand for passenger and vehicular access will undoubtedly increase significantly.

In the 1970s, the Highland Transport Board recommended the introduction of a vehicle ferry between Lyness, Flotta and St Margaret's Hope, thereby giving a more direct access to a short crossing to Caithness via Burwick and opening up a circular tourist route. Should traffic develop substantially, there may be a case for creating a more direct and frequent vehicle ferry link between Houton and the nearest Hoy landfall at either Lyrawa Bay or Chalmers Hope, generating, among other benefits, the opportunity to develop commuting. As both South Isles services shut down early in the evening, there is a case for extending operating hours to late evening.

As the current North Isles fleet is aging, Orkney Islands Council commissioned a study to look at the future inter-island ferry services and a vessel replacement policy. The conclusions suggested an upgrade rather than anything more radical.

The study suggested a possible fixed link to Shapinsay. If achieved, a further fixed link between Eday and Westray via Faray and possibly Papa Westray would yield far greater benefits in creating in effect one large island and a much shorter, cheaper and more frequent crossing between a new terminal on Shapinsay – if practicable at, say, Noust of Erraby or at Innkster – and Eday, with links to nearby Stronsay and Sanday, offering a step change in North Isles accessibility. Collectively, while the capital costs of such a programme would be substantial, ferry-operating costs would be slashed and island economies boosted.

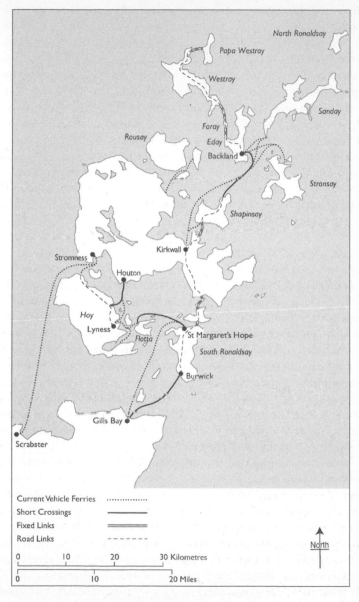

Orkney Short Crossings

Passenger-only Services

There are a number of year-round, local authority-contracted, passenger-only services, viz: Gourock–Kilcreggan; Fort William–Camusnagaul; Mallaig–Inverie–Loch Nevis. The latter is supplemented by *Spanish John* for transport of vehicles and plant. Each of these represents relatively low-cost but useful connections.

There are, however, opportunities for developing a new range of economy-enhancing passenger services based on proven technologies in common use throughout the world – namely fast passenger catamarans. Three sea areas in particular appear to offer potential. These are:

1. Sound of Sleat–Inner Sound–Sound of Raasay
2. Firth of Lorne–Sound of Mull
3. Firth of Forth

The type of vessel that would be suitable for this trade would typically have a crew of three, capacity for some 200 passengers and a service speed of around 28 knots. With their low deadweight, fast passenger catamarans give relatively good fuel economy per passenger mile and are relatively cheap to run and could open up new travel and commuting opportunities.

The once popular Skye mail steamer service from Mallaig through the Sound of Sleat to Kyle, Portree, no longer runs, although in Norway, for example, such routes are maintained by fast, economical catamarans providing links that are otherwise relatively inconvenient. A twice-daily fast boat connecting Portree with Mallaig trains would also provide convenient links with Raasay, Applecross (Toscaig), Kyle and Glenelg, otherwise difficult by public transport.

A similar arrangement is possible for the Firth of Lorne and Sound of Mull, allowing daily commuting from Mull ports and Lochaline to Oban. A fast service to Lismore would also be feasible, thereby supplementing a cheap, frequent vehicle ferry at Port Appin. Opportunities for day trips to Morvern, Tobermory or Iona by fast ferry would reduce the need for a large passenger certificate on the Oban–Craignure vehicle ferry service, thereby greatly reducing overall costs.

On the Firth of Forth, too, a fast passenger commuter Burntisland–Granton service has long been mooted with the possibility of other links to Rosyth and other Fife ports. Due to refusal of funding, recent attempts to reinstate this route have been shelved. In spring 2013, SESTRAN announced plans to support a reinstated a passenger ferry on the 'Pilgrim Route' between North Berwick (East Lothian) and Fife.

A WAY FORWARD

It will not have escaped the notice of some readers that the title of this book was inspired by Charon of Greek mythology. He ferried the souls of the dead across the rivers Styx and Acheron to the underworld. Safe passage required payment of a coin. Failure to do so condemned those unfortunates to wander the shores aimlessly for a hundred years.

It is doubly ironic that succeeding Scottish Government administrations have paid out increasing and now vast subsidies to support many of our ferry services. Yet the aimlessness exhibited by our policy makers has failed to achieve cost-effective operation of the ferry services propped up by this largesse. It is hoped that this book will inspire a more focussed approach.

The above chapters describe how many of Scotland's ferry and passenger vessel operators have been able to develop high-quality services while minimising, or avoiding altogether, the need for public subsidy. Also described are the bloated, polluting, monopolistic and secretive state-subsidised operators, not one of whose routes covers its costs from the farebox and where the styles of operation often do not adequately address the needs of the island and peninsular communities they purport to serve.

The reasons for this dichotomy are deep seated. Over the last half century every major political party has wielded ministerial power in Scotland, yet not one of them has shown the will to tackle this scandal.

On the other hand, examples of how some independent operators in Scotland and in other countries do things better have been outlined. Drawing on these lessons, suggestions have been put forward as to how Scotland's ferry services could be made much more cost-effective and less polluting, while actually improving the level of service.

The solution lies in more cost-effective and economical vehicle ferries and, in some instances, fast passenger craft, more flexible crewing and operating methods and, where possible, replacement of long, infrequent routes with short, frequent crossings or fixed road links. It is important to note, as a broad rule of thumb, that per-unit-carried-per-mile vehicle ferry operation is some ten times more costly and emits some ten times the greenhouse gases compared with a vehicle on the road.

Movement towards a better, more efficient ferry provision can best be achieved, first by making route-by-route costings available to facilitate understanding of how current inefficiencies might be addressed. In light of that, route-by-route tendering will encourage operators to come up with proposals that can be judged for cost-effectiveness, community and environmental benefit. The big change to present policy would be to reward efficiency and environmental gains rather than punish those who achieve them. In many cases no subsidy may be required at all, as demonstrated by Western Ferries and Pentland Ferries.

If the kinds of approach suggested in the last chapter of this book were adopted, the connectivity of many of our island communities would be much improved while at the same time it is calculated that annual subsidies and greenhouse gas emissions would be much reduced. That is surely an outcome that is worth striving for.

There is a good deal of work to be done in refining the way ahead, but the sooner that is done the sooner the desired improvements will be realised. If they are, Scotland could once more lead the world in maritime development.

APPENDIX 1

FERRY CROSSINGS AND TRAFFIC 2010

Traffic figures are for 2010, where available at time of writing

Passage length is shown in kilometres with fractions rounded up to the next full number

Routes	Km	Op	Passengers	Cars	CVs/ Buses
Clyde Routes					
Stranraer–Belfast	78	SL	1,084,000	244,000	98,228
Cairnryan–Larne	59	P&O	611,000	151,000	217,804
Girvan–Ailsa Craig	17	MMC			
Troon–Larne	106	P&O	225,000	62,000	27,097
Ardrossan–Brodick	19	CM	731,126	134,214	13,217
Largs–Cumbrae	2	CM	727,310	138,680	5,006
Wemyss Bay–Rothesay	11	CM	735,308	155,687	12,607
McInroy's Point–Hunter's Quay	4	WF	1,313,800	564,000	33,000
Gourock–Dunoon (now P)	7	CF	499,000	61,400	3,500
Gourock–Kilcreggan (P)	3	CMM	63,500	0	0
Renfrew–Yoker	1	CL		0	0
Colintraive–Rhubodach	1	CM	264,287	84,850	14,937
Tarbert–Portavadie	7	CM	68,095	21,242	521
Lochranza–Claonaig (S)	8	CM	52,062	16,553	526
Lochranza–Tarbert (winter)	20	CM			
Lamlash–Holy Isle (P)	3	HIF	12		
Campbelltown–Ballycastle	60	KE			
West Highlands (Argyll)					
Tayinloan–Gigha	6	CM	66,539	14,184	1,627
Kennacraig–Port Ellen/ Port Askaig	50	CM	169,280	54,239	9,800
Tayvallich–Jura (P, S)	33	ISS	2,816	0	0
Cuan	1	ABC	16,300	7,000	300

West Highlands (Argyll)–*contd*

Routes	Km	Op	Passengers	Cars	CVs/ Buses
Easdale (P)	1	ABC	15,000	0	
Gallanach–Kerrera	1	KF			
Oban–Colonsay	59	CM	16,368	4,628	300
Oban–Craignure	15	CM	564,476	108,515	11,218
Oban–Coll–Tiree	96	CM	52,241	15,643	1,809
Oban–Castlebay/Lochboisdale	144	CM	58,221	18,005	1,345
Oban–Lismore	12	CM	19,582	2,779	300
Port Appin–Lismore (P)	1	ABC	38,200	0	0

Argyll (inter-island)

Routes	Km	Op	Passengers	Cars	CVs/ Buses
Feolin–Port Askaig	1	ASP	38,200	23,900	2,600
Fionnphort–Iona	2	CM	233,194	5,218	1,031
Fionnphort–Staffa (P, S)	11	GG			
Ulva Ferry–Ulva (P)	1	DM			
Ulva Ferry–Staffa, etc. (P, S)	2	TM			

West Highlands (North)

Routes	Km	Op	Passengers	Cars	CVs/ Buses
Corran–Ardgour	1	THC	550,000	221,400	14,400
Fort William–Camasnagall (P)	2	CC	4,400	0	0
Lochaline–Fishnish	3	CM	115,620	45,259	3,831
Kilchoan–Tobermory	11	CM	34,983	5,566	17
Arisaig–Eigg, etc. (P, S)	17	AM			
Mallaig–Small Isles	74	CM	26,697	961	264
Mallaig–Armadale	8	CM	212,417	51853	1,915
Mallaig–Inverie (Knoydart) (P)	11	BW	3,000	0	0
Mallaig Freight (F)		MT			
Glenelg–Kylerea (S)	1	RM			
Elgol–Loch Coruisk (S)	7	BJ			
Elgol–Loch Coruisk (S)	7	MI			
Uig–Lochmaddy	48	CM	181,776	67,865	7,715
Uig–Tarbert	47	CM			
Raasay–Sconser	3	CM	58,043	21,189	13,000
Badluachrach–Scoraig	2	SST			
Ullapool–Stornoway	84	CM	227,676	67,583	14,128
Kyle of Druness (P, S)	1	CWF			

Western Isles (inter-island)

Routes	Km	Op	Passengers	Cars	CVs/ Buses
Ardmhor–Eriskay	27	CM	46,096	15,972	1,496
Berneray–Leverburgh	20	CM	58,020	23,660	1,496
Tarbert–Shiants (P, S)	32	SH			

Western Isles (inter-island)–*contd*

Routes	Km	Op	Passengers	Cars	CVs/ Buses
Leverburgh–St Kilda (P, S)	75	SH			
Leverburgh–St Kilda (P, S)	75	KC			
Castlebay–Kisimul Castle (S)	1	HS			
Orkney (External)					
Scrabster–Stromness	51	NL	141,640	39,571	7,557
Gills Bay–St Margaret's Hope	29	PF	97,677	34,664	6,718
John O'Groats–Burwick (P, S)	13	T&B	34,000	0	0
Aberdeen–Kirkwall	248	NL	36,000	4,900	4,600
Aberdeen–Kirkwall (F)	248	SS			
Orkney (inter-island)					
Houghton–Lyness/Flotta	11	OF	78,800	19,000	5,400
Stromness–Graemsay–Hoy	9	OF	23,100	0	0
Tingwall–Rousay/Egilsay/Wyre	11	OF	58,800	10,200	6,700
Kirkwall–Shapinsay	7	OF	64,200	7,500	4,700
Kirkwall–Stronsay/Eday	37	OF	23,500	6,200	
Stronsay–Papa Stronsay	1	GMI			
Kirkwall–Westray	30	OF	31,700	9,300	
Kirkwall–Sanday	30	OF	21,050	6,640	
Kirkwall–Papa Westray/ N Ronaldsay	57	OF	1,400	0	
Shetland (External)					
Aberdeen–Lerwick	337	NL	113,100	18,997	17,063
Aberdeen–Lerwick (F)	337	SS			
Kirkwall–Lerwick	165	NL	15,400	2,400	800
Shetland (inter-island)					
Grutness (Sumburgh)– Fair Isle (L)	41	SIC			
Sandwick–Mousa	16	TMB			
Lerwick–Fair Isle (L)	67	SIC			
Lerwick–Bressay	1	SIC	189,000	66,400	3,700
Lerwick–Skerries	37	SIC			
Vidlin–Skerries	22	SIC			
Vidlin–Symbister (Whalsay)	11	SIC			
Laxo–Symbister (Whalsay	8	SIC	164,000	72,200	4,000
Toft–Ulsta (Yell)	6	SIC	272,000	129,200	7,300
Gutcher–Belmont (Unst)	3	SIC	130,000	60,000	

Shetland (inter-island)–*contd*

Routes	Km	Op	Passengers	Cars	CVs/Buses
Gutcher–Fetlar	6	SIC			
West Burrafirth–Papa Stour (L)	8	SIC			
Walls–Foula (P)	32	BKM			
East Coast					
Nigg–Cromarty (S)	2	CFC	13,000		
Rosyth–Zeebrugge (F)	720	DFD	54,000	16,000	36,000
Queensferry–Inchcolm (P)	8	MOF			
Queensferry–Inchcolm (P)	8	FTB			
North Berwick–Anstruther (P, S) *	17	MOF			
Inland Waters					
Clansman–Urquhart Castle (P)	9	JC	150,000		
Inverness–Urquhart Castle (P, S)	23	JC			
Balloch–Balmaha (P, S)	10	SC			
Balloch–Luss (P, S)	11	SC	300,000		
Balmaha–Loch Lomond Islands (P)		MF			
Luss–Balmaha (P, S)	7	CLL			
Luss–Inchcailloch (P, S)	6	CLL			
Tarbet–Inversnaid (P, S)	6	CLL			
Tarbet–Rowardennan (P, S)	8	CLL			
Trossachs Pier–Stronachlachar (P, S)	11	LKE			
Inchmaholm (P, S)	2	HS			
Kinross–Loch Leven (P, S)	5	HS			
Threave Castle (P, S)	1	HS			
Totals	**3,851**		**10,678,300**	**2,896,217**	**583,573**

Note: (P) = passenger-only ferry; (S) = seasonal; (L) = limited vehicle capacity

Traffic included in above figure(s)

* Planned to start summer 2013

Italic figures are estimates

OPERATOR CODES   Number of Vessels

ABC – Argyll and Bute Council	3
AM – Arisaig Marine	1
ASP – ASP Ship Management Ltd	1
BJ – Bella Jane Cruises	1
BKM – B K Marine	1
BW – Bruce Watt	2
CC – Crannog Cruises	2
CF – Cowal Ferries/now Argyll Ferries	2
CFC – Cromarty Ferry Company	1
CL – Clydelink	3
CLL – Cruise Loch Lomond	6
CM – Caledonian MacBrayne	30
CMM – Clyde Marine	5
CWF – Cape Wrath Ferry	1
DFD – DFDS	1
DM – Donald Munro	1
FTB – Forth Boat Tours	1
GG – Gordon Grant Marine	4
GMI – Golgotha Monastery Island	1
HIF Holy Isle Ferry (and others)	2
HS – Historic Scotland	6
ISS – Nicol MacKinnon's Islay Sea Safari	1
JC – Jacobite Cruises	3
KC – Kilada Cruises	2
KE – Kintyre Express	1
KF – Kerrera Ferry Ltd	1
LKE – Loch Katrine Experience (The)	2
MI – Misty Isle Boat Trips	1
MF – Macfarlane & Sons	3
MMC – Mark McCrindle	1
MOF – Maid of the Forth	5
NL – NorthLink	5
OF – Orkney Ferries	9
P&O – P&O Ferries	3
PF – Pentland Ferries	1
RM – R MacLeod	1
SC – Sweeney's Cruises	4

OPERATOR CODES–*contd*	Number of Vessels
SH – Sea Harris	1
SIC – Shetland Isles Council	12
SS – Streamline Shipping	1
SST – Scoraig Sea Taxis	1
T&B – Thomas & Bews	1
THC – Highland Council	2
TM – Turus Mara	2
TMB – The Mousa Boat	1
WF – Western Ferries	4
TOTAL	**143**

FLEET LISTS 2013

Name (build year)	Type	Date Aqu'rd	Length (m)	Power (kW)	Crew	Pax	Cars	Normal Route
FERRY OPERATORS								
Argyll and Bute Council								
Belnahua	VF					40	6	Cuan
Torsa	P						0	Cuan
(boat)	P						0	Easdale
Lismore	P				2	20	0	Lismore
Arisaig Marine								
Shearwater	P	1998			2	89	0	Arisaig–Eigg
ASP Ship Management								
Eilean Dhiura	VF	1998					10	Feolin
Argyll Ferries								
Ali Cat (2000)	Pcat	2011	19.50		4	250	0	Dunoon
Argyll Flier (2001)	P	2011	26.00	1582	4	188	0	Dunoon
Bella Jane Cruises								
Bella Jane	P	1992	12	471	2	40	0	Elgol–L. Coruisk
BK Marine								
New Advance	PFF	2008	9.80			12	1	Foula
Caledonian MacBrayne Ferries								
Eigg	VF(B)	1974	22.50	220	3	164	6	Lismore
Raasay	VF(B)	1976	22.50	220	3	75	6	Reserve vessel
Isle of Cumbrae	VF(D)	1976	38.00	310	3	160	18	Portavadie
Saturn	RoPax	1977	69.50	1796	10	510	40	Brodick

Name (build year)	Type	Date Aqu'rd	Length (m)	Power (kW)	Crew	Pax	Cars	Normal Route
FERRY OPERATORS–*contd*								
Caledonian MacBrayne Ferries–*contd*								
Isle of Arran	RoPax	1983	84.92	3450	20	448	76	Reserve vessel
Hebridean Isles	RoPax	1985	85.17	3450	24	510	64	Islay
Loch Striven	VF(D)	1986	35.51	540	3	203	12	Raasay
Loch Linnhe	VF(D)	1986	35.51	540	3	203	12	Kilchoan
Loch Riddon	VF(D)	1986	35.51	540	3	203	12	Cumbrae
Loch Ranza	VF(D)	1987	35.51	540	3	203	12	Gigha
Isle of Mull	RoPax	1987	90.30	6800	28	962	70	Craignure
Lord of the Isles	RoPax	1989	84.60	4320	28	506	56	Tiree/Colonsay
Loch Dunvegan	VF(D)	1991	73.80	660	4	250	36	Colintraive
Loch Fyne	VF(D)	1991	73.80	660	4	250	36	Fishnish
Loch Buie	VF(D)	1992	34.50	490	4	250	10	Iona
Loch Tarbert	VF(D)	1992	34.50	460	3	150	18	Lochranza
Caledonian Isles	RoPas	1993	94.00	4326	26	1000	110	Brodick
Isle of Lewis	RoPax	1995	101.25	6532	32	680	123	Stornoway
Loch Bhrusda	VF(D)	1996	35.40	1188	3	150	18	Relief vessel
Loch Alainn	VF(D)	1997	41.00	970	4	150	24	Sound of Barra
Clansman	RoPax	1998	99.00	7650	28	638	90	Barra
Hebrides	RoPax	2000	99.40	7650	33	612	90	Uig
Lochnevis	VF(S)	2001	49.20	1890	10	190	14	Small Isles
Muirneag (1979)	ROF	2002	105.50	3900		12		Stornoway
Loch Portain	VF(D)	2003	49.95	2236		200	36	Sound of Harris
Coruisk	VF(D)	2003	65.00	2280	6	250	40	Armadale
Bute	RoPax	2005	72.00	2960	10	450	60	Rothesay
Argyll	RoPax	2006	72.00	2960	10	450	60	Rothesay
Loch Shira	VF(D)	2007	53.90	1120		250	36	Cumbrae
Finlaggan	RoPax	2011	89.80	8000	21	550	85	Islay
Hallaig	VF(D)	2013	43.50	750	3	150	23	Raasay
Lochinvar	VF(D)	2013	43.50	750	3	150	23	Portavadie
Loch Seaforth (building)	RoPax		116.00			700	143	Stornoway
Clydelink								
Island Princess	P	2012				96	0	Kilcreggan
Cromarty Ferry Company								
Cromarty Queen	VF(B)	2010	17.25	338	2	47	4	Cromarty

Name (build year)	Type	Date Aqu'rd	Length (m)	Power (kW)	Crew	Pax	Cars	Normal Route
FERRY OPERATORS–*contd*								
Cruise Loch Lomond	P							
Lomond Princess	P	1978				52	0	Loch Lomond
Lomond Prince	P					126	0	Loch Lomond
Lomond Laird	P					48	0	Loch Lomond
Lomond Chieftain	P					80	0	Loch Lomond
Lomond Queen	P					80	0	Loch Lomond
Lomond Warrior	P					25	0	Loch Lomond
Cruise Loch Ness								
Royal Scot	P	1991	16.50	220		120	0	Loch Ness
Caledonian Spirit (1997)	P	2012	13.00	258		96	0	Loch Ness
Ness Express	RIB		10.00	232		12	0	Loch Ness
Ness Explorer	RIB		10.00	232		12	0	Loch Ness
Elgol Boat Trips								
Sea Eagle	P	2012	8.00			12	0	Elgol–L. Coruisk
Forth Boat Tours								
Forth Belle	P		25.30			115	0	Inchcolm
Gordon Grant Marine								
Ossian of Staffa	P	1993			2	65	0	Iona–Staffa, etc
Ullin of Staffa	P	2000			2	85	0	Iona–Staffa, etc
Islander	P	2011			2	65	0	Iona–Staffa, etc
Lady Iona (2007)	P	2010			2	86	0	Glensanda
Highland Council, The								
Maid of Glencoul	VF(D)	1976	32.00	404		116	17	Reserve vessel
Corran	VF(D)	2007	42	942		150	30	Corran
Historic Scotland	P							
(motor boat)	P				1	12	0	Kisimul Castle
(motor boat)	P				1	12	0	Inchmahome
(motor boat)	P				1	12	0	Loch Leven
(motor boat)	P				1	6	0	Threave Castle
Isle of Skye Ferry CIC								
Glenachulish	VF(T)				2	12	6	Kylerea

Name (build year)	Type	Date Aqu'rd	Length (m)	Power (kW)	Crew	Pax	Cars	Normal Route
FERRY OPERATORS–*contd*								
Jacobite Cruises								
Jacobite Queen (1949)	P	1987	22.86			159	0	Loch Ness
Jacobite Legend	P	2006	26.27	195		100	0	Loch Ness
Jacobite Warrior	PCat	2012	24.50			250	0	Loch Ness
Kilda Cruises (Atlantic Marine Services)								
Orca II	P	2007	16.78			12	0	St Kilda
Orca III	PCat	2012	17.00	1030	3	12	0	St Kilda
Loch Katrine Experience (The)								
Sir Walter Scott (1900)	P	2006	34.00		5	200	0	Loch Katrine
Lady of the Lake	P		17.70					Loch Katrine
Loch Shiel Cruises								
Sileas (1940)	P	1996	15.86		2	50	0	Loch Shiel
Mark McCrindle								
Glorious	P					12	0	Ailsa Craig
Macfarlane & Sons								
Marion	P		12.00		2	36		Loch Lomond
Margaret	P		9.15		2	26		Loch Lomond
Maid of the Forth								
Maid of the Forth	P	1988	19.00		5	225	0	Inchcolm
Safari Explorer	PCat	2013		660		57		N. Berwick–Fife
RIB Inchcolm	RIB		11.00	440	2	12	0	Newhaven
Seabird One	RIB		10.00	368	2	12	0	Bass, Isle of May
Seabird Two	RIB		10.00	368	2	12	0	Bass, Isle of May
Seabird Three	P	2011			2	12	0	Bass
Miligan Transport								
Spanish John	VFF(B)	2003	18.00	339	3	12	6	Freight charter
Misty Isle Boat Trips								
Misty Isle (1966)	P	2005	12.50	110	2	63	0	Elgol–L. Coruisk
Mousa Boat (The)								
Solan IV	P	1999				60	0	Mousa

Name (build year)	Type	Date Aqu'rd	Length (m)	Power (kW)	Crew	Pax	Cars	Normal Route
FERRY OPERATORS–*contd*								
Orkney Ferries								
Earl Thorfinn	VF	1989	45.00	1489		190	25	North Isles
Earl Sigurd	VF	1989	45.00	1469		190	25	North Isles
Varagan (1989)	VF	1991	50.00	1580		144	32	North Isles
Hoy Head	VF	1994	53.00	740		125		South Isles
Shapinsay	VF(B)	1988	27.00	540		91	11	Shapinsay
Eynhallow	VF(B)	1987	29.00	441		95	9	Rousay
Thorsvoe	VF(B)	1991	35.00	692				reserve vessel
Graemsay	PFF	1996	20.50	448		73	1	Graemsay
Golden Mariana (1973)	P	1987	15.25	97		140	0	Papa Westray
P&O Ferries								
European Causeway	ROPax	2000	156.20	31680	55	410	375	Larne
European Highlander	ROPax	2002	162.70	31680	55	410	375	Larne
Express (1998)	HSVcat	2005	91.00	28800		900	240	Larne
Pentland Ferries								
Pentalina	VCat	2008	64	3,876	10 or11	250	78	St Mgt Hope
Scoraig Sea Taxis								
Clan Albain	PCat	2011		60	1	12	0	Scoraig
Sea Harris								
Enchanted Isle	P	2005	12.81	515	2	12	0	St Kilda
Serco NorthLink Ferries								
Hjaltland	RoPax	2002	125	21600	37	600	125	Abdn, Ork, Shet
Hrossey	RoPax	2002	125.00	21600	37	600	125	Abdn, Ork, Shet
Hamnavoe	RoPax	2002	112.00	86800	28 to 40	600	96	Stromness
Hildasay (1999)	ROF	2010	122.30	7400	12			Ork/Shet freight
Helliear (1997)	ROF	2010	122.00	7400	12			Ork/Shet freight
Shetland Islands Council								
Thora	VF	1975	23.15	262	4	93	10	relief vessel
Hendra	VF	1982	33.60	750	5	55	14	Whalsay
Snolda	VF(S)	1983	49.56	445	4or5	12	6	Papa Stour
Fivla	VF	1985	30.00	656	4	95	12	relief vessel
Good Shepherd	PFF	1986	18.30	239	4	12	2	Fair Isle

Name (build year)	Type	Date Aqu'rd	Length (m)	Power (kW)	Crew	Pax	Cars	Normal Route
FERRY OPERATORS–*contd*								
Shetland Islands Council–*contd*								
Geira	VF	1988	30.00	656	4or5	50	12	Bluemull
Bigga	VF	1991	33.00	728	4	96	16	Bluemull
Leirna	VF(D)	1992	32.45	500	4or5	124	20	Bressay
Linga	VF	2002	36.21	920	5	95	16	Whalsay
Filla	VF(S)	2003	35.50	1342	5	29	9	Skerries
Daggri	VF(D)	2004	65.36	2400	5or6	95	31	Yell Sound
Dagalein	VF(D)	2004	65.36	2400	5or6	95	31	Yell Sound
Streamline Shipping								
Daroja (1997)	CS	2006	91.00	3520		0	0	Ork/Shet freight
Stena Sealink								
Stena Superfast VIII (2001)	ROPax	2011	203.30	46,000	63	661	626	Belfast
Srena Superfast VII (2001)	ROPax	2011	203.90	46,000	63	661	626	Belfast
Summer Queen Cruises								
Summer Queen (1972)	P	c1985				158	0	Summer Isles
Sweeny's Cruises								
Lomond Duchess	P						0	Loch Lomond
Silver Marlin	P	1992				120	0	Loch Lomond
Astina	P	2004				150	0	Loch Lomond
Silver Dolphin	P	2009				90	0	Loch Lomond
Turus Mara								
Island Lass (1967)	P	1995	14.00	162	2	69	0	Staffa, Treshnish
Hoy Lass (1975)	P	1995	15.25	471	2	63	0	Staffa, Treshnish
Western Ferries								
Sound of Scalpay (1961)	VF(D)	1995	47.00	716	4	37	220	Cowal
Sound of Sanda (1963)	VF(D)	1996	47.00	716	4	37	220	Cowal
Sound of Scarba	VF(D)	2001	50.00	880	4	45	220	Cowal
Sound of Shuna	VF(D)	2003	50.00	882	4	45	220	Cowal
Sound of Seil (building)	VF(D)	2013	50.00	900	4	40	220	Cowal
Sound of Soay (building)	VF(D)	2013	50.00	900	4	40	220	Cowal

CRUISE AND CHARTER OPERATORS

Name (build year)	Type	Date Aqu'rd	Length (m)	Power (kW)	Crew	Pax	Cars	Normal Route
Clyde Marine Motoring Co Ltd								
Rover	P	1964	19.8			80	0	Firth of Clyde
Cruiser	P	1974	24	224		200	0	Firth of Clyde
Fencer	P	1976	11	95		30	0	Aberdeen Harb.
Seabus	P	2007	19.5			100	0	Firth of Clyde
Clyde Clipper	PCat	2010	27	803		250	0	Firth of Clyde
Cruise Loch Ness								
Royal Scot	P	1991	16.50	220		120	0	Loch Ness
Caledonian Spirit (1997)	P	2012	13.00	258		96	0	Loch Ness
Ness Express	RIB		10.00	232		12	0	Loch Ness
Ness Explorer	RIB		10.00	232		12	0	Loch Ness
Hebridean Island Cruises								Highlands and
Hebridean Princess (1964)	P	1988	71.63	35	38	49	0	Isles
Magna Carta Steamship Co. Ltd								Caledonian
Lord of the Glens	P	2000	41.61	588		54	0	Canal
Majestic Line								
Glen Massan	P	2004	24.00			11	0	West Highlands
Glen Tarsan	P	2007	24.00			11	0	West Highlands
Waverley Steam Navigation Co.								
Waverley (1947)	P		73.13			950	0	Firth of Clyde

CS – Container ship
HSVcat – High-speed, vehicle–carrying catamaran
PCat – Passenger catamaran
PFF – Passenger and freight ferry
P – Passenger vessel
RIB – Rigid-hulled inflatable boat
ROF – RO–RO freighter
ROPax – Large RO–RO passenger and vehicle ferry
VF – Vehicle ferry(bow and stern loading)
VF(B) – Vehicle ferry (bow loading)
VF(D) – Vehicle ferry (double ended)
VF(S) – Vehicle ferrry, stern loading
VF(T) – Vehicle ferry, turntable

APPENDIX 3

CALEDONIAN MACBRAYNE LOSSES BY ROUTE 2006

	2007	2007	2011
		(£ per pax return)	
	(£k)	Actual	Computed
Gourock–Dunoon	2,500		
Wemyss Bay–Rothesay	3,390	9.22	17.53
Largs Cumbrae	922	2.54	4.82
Colintraive–Rhubodach	650	4.92	9.36
Tarbert–Portavadie	280	8.24	15.65
Oban–Castlebay–Lochboisdale	4,464	153.93	292.47
Ullapool–Stornoway	4,607	40.41	76.78
Oban–Coll–Tiree	1,576	60.62	115.17
Uig–Tarbert/Lochmaddy	3,389	37.45	71.15
Berneray–Leverburgh	770	26.55	50.45
Barra–Eriskay	449	19.52	37.09
Kennacraig–Islay	4,462	52.80	100.33
Tayinloan–Gigha	357	10.66	20.25
Oban–Craignure	1,842	6.53	12.41
Fishnish–Lochaline	267	4.60	8.75
Tobermory–Kilchoan	505	28.86	54.83
Oban–Lismore	314	31.40	59.66
Fionnphort–Iona	572	4.91	9.33
Mallaig–Armadale	643	6.07	11.53

Mallaig–Small Isles	1,828	135.41	257.27
Raasay–Sconser	720	24.83	47.17
Oban–Colonsay	1,012	126.50	240.35
Ardrossan–Brodick	1,582	4.33	8.22
Lochranza–Cloanaig	182	7.00	13.30
Total subsidy for routes shown	37,283		

Source: Scottish Government.

Note: 2007 is the last year for which deficits by route have been made available. As overall subsidy levels for 2011 are approximately 90 per cent higher than 2007, per-passenger (return journey) estimated values for 2010 have been extrapolated on that basis pro rata from the passenger carryings as set out in Appendix 1. For subsidy per single passenger journey, the values shown should be halved.

APPENDIX 4

SUBSIDY ESTIMATES PER HEAD OF POPULATION FOR SELECTED ISLANDS

	Population	£ per head
Bute	7,228	3561
Cumbrae	1,434	1,222
Arran	5,058	1,650
Barra and South Uist	2,990	3,206
Lewis	17,900	489
Coll and Tiree	934	3,206
Harris, North Uist and Benbecula	4,500	1,434
Islay	3,457	2,452
Gigha	110	6,166
Mull	2,808	2,023
Lismore (excluding Port Appin)	146	4,086
Iona	125	8,694
Small Isles	131	26,523
Raasay	192	7,125
Colonsay	108	17,804

Note: the above values are notional and are calculated from a combination of the 2001 census population figures for each island or group of islands, and the estimated 2011 route deficit figures as extrapolated from Appendix 3.

APPENDIX 5

FIXED LINKS

Listed below are fixed links built to replace ferry or shipping services in Scotland since the outbreak of the Second World War

Dornie
  1940 Dornie Bridge (replaced 1990)
  1942 South Ford Bridge (South Uist–Benbecula) (replaced 1983)
  1945 Churchill Barriers (Orkney Mainland–South Ronaldsay)
  1953 Great Bernera Bridge (Lewis)
  1960 North Ford Causeway between Benbecula and North Uist
  1962 Baleshare Causeway (North Uist)
  1963 Clyde Tunnel (northbound)
  1964 Clyde Tunnel (southbound)
  1964 Forth Road Bridge
  1966 Tay Road Bridge
  1966 Connel Bridge (replacing Boneawe Ferry)
  1970 Stromeferry Bypass*
  1971 Erskine Bridge
  1971 Kyle of Tongue Bridge/causeway
  1971 Trondra and Burra Bridges (Shetland)
  1975 Ballachulish Bridge
  1982 Kessock Bridge
  1984 Kylesku Bridge
  1991 Vatersay Causeway
  1995 Skye Bridge
  1997 Scalpay Bridge (Harris)
  1999 Berneray Causeway (North Uist)
  2001 Eriskay Causeway

Note: *In October 2008 loose rocks made the Stromeferry Bypass roads unsafe and a temporary ferry service provided alternative access during repair works. In January 2012 a further series of rockfalls closed the road. Highland Council chartered two vessels to provide a temporary ferry service. The 61-seater cruise boat *Sula Mhor* carried school pupils and other foot passengers from the Lochcarron and Applecross areas to Plockton. The six-vehicle turntable ferry MV *Glenachulish* that normally operated the summer-only Glenelg–Kylerhea ferry service was pressed into service between the old ferry slipways at Stromeferry and North Strome, thereby avoiding a 140-mile (230km) road detour.

BIBLIOGRAPHY

BOOKS

Aitken, John, *Above the Tay Bridges*, Montrose, 1986

Anderson, Iain F., *To Introduce the Hebrides*, London, 1933

Bannerman, Gry and Patricia, *The Ships of British Columbia*, Surrey BC, 1985

Bell, J.J., *Scotland's Rainbow West*, London, 1933

Bent Mike, *Steamers of the Fjords: Bergen Shipping since 1839*, London, 1989

Blue, Arthur, *The Sound of Sense*, Glasgow, undated

Brodie, Ian, *Steamers of the Forth*, Newton Abbot, 1976

Brown, Alan, *Loch Lomond Passenger Steamers 1818–1989*, Nuneaton, 2000

Bryant, John, *Hurtigruten 120*, Ramsey, Isle of Man, 2013

Castle, Colin, *A Legacy of Fame: Shipping and Shipbuilding on the Clyde*, Erskine, 1990

Clark, Andrew, *A World Apart: The Story of Hebridean Shipping*, Catrine, 2010

Cleg, Peter V., *A Flying Start to the Day*, Godalming, 1986

Cormack, Alastair and Anne, *Days of Orkney Steam*, Kirkwall, 1971

Correia, Luís Miguel, *Cacilheiros*, Lisbon, 1996

Donaldson, Gordon, *A Northern Commonwealth*, Edinburgh 1990

Donaldson, Gordon, *Northwards by Sea*, Edinburgh, 1966

Deayton, Alistair, *MacBrayne Steamers*, Stroud, 2011

Deayton, Alistair, *Orkney and Shetland Steamers*, Stroud, 2002

Deayton, Alistair and Iain Quinn, *A MacBrayne Album*, Amberley, 2009

Duckworth, C.L.D. and Langmuir, G.E.L., *Clyde and Other Coastal Steamers*, Prescot 1977

Duckworth, C.L.D. and Langmuir, G.E.L., *Clyde River and Other Steamers*, Glasgow 1972

Duckworth, .CL.D. and Langmuir, G.E.L., *West Highland Steamers*, Prescot, 1967

Gardiner, *Stage Coach to John O'Groats*, London, 1961

Haldane, A.R.B., *The Drove Roads of Scotland*, Edinburgh, 1952

Haldane, A.R.B., *New Ways through the Glens*, Edinburgh, 1962

Haldane, A.R.B., *Three Centuries of Scottish Posts*, Edinburgh, 1971

Hendy, John, *Ferries of Scotland*, Kilgetty, undated

Hughes, Lt-Colonel Henry, *Immortal Sails*, Prescot, 1977

Linklater, Eric, *Orkney and Shetland*, London, 1965

McCrorie, Ian, *To the Coast: One Hundred Years of the Caledonian Steam Packet Co.*, Fairlie, 1989

McCrorie, Ian, *The Sea Route to Islay: The Journey to Finlaggan*, Port Glasgow, undated

McCrorie, Ian, *Royal Road to the Isles*, Gourock, undated

McCrorie, Ian, *Caledonian MacBrayne: Ships of the Fleet*, Ramsey, Isle of Man, 1980

McLean, Gavin, *A Century of Shipping in New Zealand*, Wellington, 2000

McQueen, Andrew, *Echoes of Old Clyde Paddle Wheels*, Glasgow, 1924

McQueen, Andrew *Clyde River Steamers of the Last Fifty Years*, Glasgow, 1923

Meek, Donald E. and Peter, Bruce, *From Comet to CalMac*, Ramsey, Isle of Man, 2011

Milbe, Peter, *ABC Clyde Steamers and Loch Lomond Fleets in and after 1936*, London, undated

Miller, James, *A Wild and Open Sea*, Kirkwall, 1994

Musk, George, *Canadian Pacific: The Story of a Famous Shipping Line*, Newton Abbot, 1989

Neal, Carolyn and Thomas Kilday Janus, *Puget Sound Ferries*, Sun Valley CA, 2001

Ordnance Survey Atlas of Great Britain, London, 1982

Pálsson, Herman and Edwards, Paul, *Orkneyinga Saga*, London, 1981

Patterson, Alan J.S., *The Golden Years of the Clyde Steamer 1989–1914*, Newton Abbot, 1969

Patterson, Alan J.S., *The Victorian Summer of the Clyde Steamer 1864–1888*, Newton Abbot, 1972

Patterson, Len, *Twelve Hundred Miles for Thirty Shillings*, Edinburgh, 1988

Patton, Brian, *A MacBrayne Memoir*, Foulden, 2009

Patton, Brian, *Irish Sea Shipping*, Kettering, 2007

Patton, Brian, *Scottish Coastal Steamers 1918–1975*, Peterborough, 1996

Pedersen, Roy N., *Loch Ness with Jacobite*, Inverness, 2007

Pedersen, Roy N., *Pentland Hero: The Saga of the Orkney Short Sea Crossing*, Edinburgh, 2010

Riddel, John, *The Clyde*, Fairlie, 1988

Robins, Nick, *The Last Steamers*, Portishead, 2005

Robins, Nick S. and Meek, Donald E., *The Kingdom of MacBrayne*, Edinburgh 2006

Rushton, Gerald A., *Whistle up the Inlet*, Vancouver BC, 1974

Rushton, Gerald, *Echoes of the Whistle: An Illustrated History of the Union Steamship Company*, Vancouver BC, 1989

Smith, Colin J., *In Fair Weather and in Foul, 30 Years of Scottish Passenger Ships and Ferries*, Narbeth, 1999

Somerville, Cameron, *Colour on the Clyde*, Rothesay, undated

Spalding, Andrea and David and Lawrence Pitt, *BC Ferries*, Vancouver BC, 1996

Stein, Alan J, *Safe Passage – The Birth of Washington State Ferries*, Seattle, 2001

Thomas, John, *British Railways Steamers of the Clyde*, London, 1948

Uncles, Christopher J, *Last Ferry to Skye*, Ochiltree, 1995

Weir, Marie, *Ferries in Scotland*, Edinburgh, 1988

Weyndling, Walter, *West Coast Tales*, Edinburgh, 2005

Williamson, Captain James, *Clyde Passenger Steamers 1812–1901*, Greenock, 1904

Wilson, Andrew, *The Sound of Silence, Subsidy and Competition in West Coast Shipping*, Glasgow, undated

Wilson, Andrew, *The Sound of the Clam*, Glasgow, undated

Wilson, Roy, *Passenger Steamers of the Glasgow and South Western Railway*, Truro, 1991

ARTICLES, REPORTS, PAMPHLETS, ETC.

Argyll Ferries Ltd, Directors' Report and Financial Statements for the Year Ended 31 March 2012

Bradshaw's Railway Guide, various issues

British Railways, Clyde Coast and Loch Lomond Steamer Services (various timetables)

Caledonian MacBrayne Annual Reports

Caledonian MacBrayne brochures and timetables

Caledonian Steam Packet Company brochures and timetables

CalMac Ferries, Directors' Report and Financial Statements for the Year Ended 31 March 2012

Clyde River Steamer Club Reviews

Commission of the European Communities, Commission Decision of 28.10.2009 on the state aid No C 16/2008 (ex NN 105/2005 and NN 35/2007) implemented by the United Kingdom of Great Britain and Northern Ireland subsidies to CalMac and NorthLink for maritime transport services in Scotland

David MacBrayne Annual Reports

David MacBrayne, timetables, various

Department of Agriculture and Fisheries for Scotland, *Report of the Highland Transport Board*, Edinburgh, 1967

Ferjeutvalget in Møre og Romsdal, Instilling av 15 Desember 1963, Molde 1963

Financial Times, 'Brussels to Probe Scottish Ferry Subsidies', London, 2008

Hall, Ian, *Western Ferries, Clyde Steamers No. 32* Summer 1996

Herald, various issues

HIDB Ferry Policy for the Highlands and Islands Consultative Draft, Inverness, 1948

Highlands and Islands Development Board, *A Ferry for Orkney*, Inverness, 1969

Highlands and Islands Development Board, *The Norse Way: a Study of Norwegian Ferry Operations*, Transport Research Paper 1, 1977

Highlands and Islands Development Board, *Occasional Bulletin 6, Highlands and Islands Transport Review*, Inverness, 1975

Highlands and Islands Development Board, *Roads to the Isles – a study of sea freight charges in the Highlands and Islands of Scotland*, Inverness, 1974

HMSO, *Passenger Fares and Freight Charges of the North of Scotland*, Orkney and Shetland Shipping Company Limited, London, 1968

HMSO, *Transport Services in the Highlands and Islands*, London, 1963

Ileach, various issues

Liddle, L.H., 'Northern "Saints"', *Sea Breezes* magazine, May and June 1960

LMS, CSPCo. and Williamson-Buchannan Steamers (1936) Ltd, Timetable of Clyde Coast Steamer Sailings and Excursions, 1937

Maritime Research Group, Napier University Transport Research Institute, *Future Options for Northern Isles Ferry Services*, Edinburgh, January 2006

MDS Transmodal, Gills Harbour Study, Chester, 1993

Møre og Romsdal Fylkesbåtar Ferjeruter, various years

Møre og Romsdal Fylkesbåtar Annual Report and Accounts, various years

MRF Report – a translation of *Ferjeutvalget in Møre og Romsdal, Instilling av 15 Desember fra Ferjeutvalget in Møre og Romsdal*, (HIDB Transport Research paper 4), Inverness, 1978

Murray's Timetables 1949 (bound set)

Northern Maritime Corridor (NMC) Project Group Report, EU Interreg IIIB, Brussels 2006

NorthLink Ferries brochures

NorthLink Ferries Ltd Directors' Report and Financial Statements for the Year Ended 31 March 2012

North of Scotland Orkney & Shetland Shipping Co brochures and sailing lists

Orcadian, various Issues

Orkney Steam Navigation Co., sailing lists, various issues

P&O Ferries brochures

Pedersen, Roy N., *A Better Way to Run Ferries, Response to the Inquiry into Ferry Services in Scotland*, Inverness 2008

Pedersen, Roy N , *Ferry Futures*, Inverness, 1999

Pedersen Consulting, *Response to Scottish Government's Ferries Review Consultation*, 2010

Pentland Ferries brochures

Press and Journal, various issues

Rogaland Trafikkselskap, Rutehefte, 2002

Rutebok for Norge, various issues

Samferdsels Departementet, Budjetterminen 1977, Oslo, 1976

Samferdsels Departementet, NOU 21: Støtteordninger I norsk samferdsel, Oslo, 1975

Samferdsels Departementet, NOU 37: Riksvegferjer, Oslo, 1977

Samferdsels Departementet, NOU 50: Standardisering av ferjer, Oslo, 1974

Scotsman, various issues

Scottish Executive, *Proposals for Tendering Clyde and Hebrides Lifeline Ferry Services*, 2002

Scottish Executive, *Scotland's National Transport Strategy, a Consultation*, 2006

Scottish Executive, *Scotland's Transport Future: Guidance on Regional Transport Strategies*, 2006

Scottish Government Ferries Review, various documents and work packages

Scottish Transport Annual Reports, various

Shetland News, various issues

Statens Vegvessen, Vegdirectoratet Ferjestastistikk, various years

Stornoway Gazette, various issues

Summer Tours in Scotland: Glasgow to the Highlands: David MacBrayne Steamers, various issues

Sunday Herald, various issues

Transport Scotland, Scottish Ferry Services Strategic Environmental Assessment

Transport Scotland, Scottish Ferry Services Ferries Plan (2013–2022)

Western Ferries timetables

West Highland Free Press, various issues

INDEX

Note: ship names are shown in *italics*. No differentiation is made between ships of the same name